Don't Take It Personally

Don't Take It Personally

Personalness and Impersonality in Social Life

EVIATAR ZERUBAVEL

OXFORD
UNIVERSITY PRESS

Oxford University Press is a department of the University of Oxford. It furthers the University's objective of excellence in research, scholarship, and education by publishing worldwide. Oxford is a registered trade mark of Oxford University Press in the UK and certain other countries.

Published in the United States of America by Oxford University Press
198 Madison Avenue, New York, NY 10016, United States of America.

© Eviatar Zerubavel 2024

All rights reserved. No part of this publication may be reproduced, stored in a retrieval system, or transmitted, in any form or by any means, without the prior permission in writing of Oxford University Press, or as expressly permitted by law, by license, or under terms agreed with the appropriate reproduction rights organization. Inquiries concerning reproduction outside the scope of the above should be sent to the Rights Department, Oxford University Press, at the address above.

You must not circulate this work in any other form and you must impose this same condition on any acquirer.

Library of Congress Cataloging-in-Publication Data
Names: Zerubavel, Eviatar, author.
Title: Don't take it personally : personalness and impersonality in social life / Eviatar Zerubavel.
Description: New York, NY : Oxford University Press, [2024] | Includes bibliographical references and index. |
Identifiers: LCCN 2023027561 (print) | LCCN 2023027562 (ebook) | ISBN 9780197691342 (paperback) | ISBN 9780197691335 (hardback) | ISBN 9780197691366 (epub) | ISBN 9780197691373
Subjects: LCSH: Individualism. | Personalism. | Social interaction. | Social perception.
Classification: LCC HM1276 .Z47 2024 (print) | LCC HM1276 (ebook) | DDC 302.5/4—dc23/eng/20230710
LC record available at https://lccn.loc.gov/2023027561
LC ebook record available at https://lccn.loc.gov/2023027562

DOI: 10.1093/oso/9780197691335.001.0001

Paperback printed by Marquis Book Printing, Canada
Hardback printed by Bridgeport National Bindery, Inc., United States of America

To Yael, without whose encouragement this book might not have been written

Contents

Preface	ix
1. "Who" Versus "What"	1
Specific ("Who") Personhood	3
Generic ("What") Personhood	7
Sociology and Impersonality	10
2. "Who" Versus "How Many"	12
Social Arithmetic	12
Quotas	15
Political Arithmetic	16
Social Fractions	19
3. The Anatomy of Impersonality	22
Social Identity	22
Typicality	26
Standardness	27
Substitutability	29
4. Impersonalization	32
Typification	32
Standardization	34
Institutionalization	36
Substitution	38
Anonymization	43
Dispassion	46
5. Modernity and Impersonality	51
Rationalism	52
Urbanism	53
Capitalism	55
Automation	58

viii CONTENTS

6. Impersonality and Its Discontents 61
   Stability and Predictability 61
   Dehumanization 64
   Personalization 69

Notes 75
Bibliography 85
Index 95

Preface

This book was conceived on the morning of November 5, 2020, as I was preparing to teach a "Classical Sociological Theory" class that was to feature a major sociological phenomenon that had fascinated me for more than four decades,[1] namely the inherent tension between our personal and impersonal visions of personhood.

But it was the extra-academic, ultimately political nature of that particular moment that led me to decide to write this book. Only two nights earlier I watched the returns of a historic U.S. presidential election featuring two diametrically contrasting fundamental visions of political authority. On one side was the sitting president, Donald Trump, whose entire re-election campaign revolved around himself personally, while on the other was Joe Biden, who focused instead on the *institution* of the presidency. Whereas Trump emphasized his singularity, Biden presented himself as a prospective heir to a forty-five-person figurative "line" of occupants of that *position*, thereby highlighting the latter's pronouncedly impersonal character.

Having just published a couple of weeks earlier a book about the fundamental theoretico-methodological tension between studying the specific and the generic,[2] I was particularly sensitized to the somewhat parallel tension between our personal and impersonal visions of personhood. That tension further deepened during the following two months, as Trump refused to concede his defeat, leading to his historically unprecedented violent attempt to decertify the official election results. Then, on January 23, 2021, three days after Biden's inauguration, I began writing this book.

Yet while cheering the triumph of impersonal law over personal charisma, I have also long been aware of impersonality's equally obvious discontents, so perfectly captured by my almost visceral response to the often-patronizing common expressions "It's nothing personal" and "Don't take it personally." I also feel deeply annoyed at receiving

X PREFACE

telemarketing "robocalls" or trying to reason with an automated "customer representative."

I am particularly indebted to James Cook, Iddo Tavory, Asia Friedman, Tom DeGloma, Gabrielle LaFleur, Ira Cohen, Juliana Horst, Armani Beck, Tali Jaffe-Dax, Natalia Ruiz-Junco, Wayne Brekhus, Hana Wirth-Nesher, Steph Peña-Alves, and Tzipy Lazar-Shoef, who read an early version of the book and discussed it with me. I have benefited tremendously from many very helpful comments I received from them.

Lastly, the book was greatly inspired by countless conversations with my lifelong companion Yael, who so compellingly encouraged me to write it. As such, I dedicate it to her.

East Brunswick, New Jersey, March 2023

1
"Who" Versus "What"

> The sociologist is concerned with *King* John, not with King *John*.
>
> —Lewis A. Coser, *Masters of Sociological Thought*, 180

In her perfectly titled romantic drama *Sir*, filmmaker Rohena Gera sensitively recounts the subtly evolving relationship between wealthy Mumbai architect Ashwin and his live-in maid Ratna. The two become increasingly closer, even exchanging personal gifts, yet Ratna nevertheless insists on calling Ashwin *Sir* despite his repeated protests ("How long are you going to call me *Sir*?" "Please don't call me that"). Their growing mutual affection notwithstanding, India's extremely rigid class distinctions effectively prevent Ratna from venturing to cross the strict traditional social barrier separating them from each other, and she ultimately quits her job and moves out of Ashwin's apartment. The film ends, however, with her hesitantly picking up her ringing cell phone, hearing Ashwin's voice, and after a long, resounding silence finally uttering his name.

The subtle yet unmistakably fundamental socio-semiotic contrast between using someone's title and his or her proper name is likewise highlighted by the following exchange between President Andrew Shepherd and his chief of staff as well as old buddy A. J. MacInerney in Rob Reiner and Aaron Sorkin's *The American President*:

AJM: Good night, *Mr. President*.
AS: A. J., . . .
AJM: Yes, sir.
AS: When we are out of the office and alone, you can call me *Andy*.
AJM: I beg your pardon . . .

Don't Take It Personally. Eviatar Zerubavel, Oxford University Press. © Eviatar Zerubavel 2024.
DOI: 10.1093/oso/9780197691335.003.0001

2 DON'T TAKE IT PERSONALLY

AS: You were the best man in my wedding, for crying out loud. Call me *Andy*.

AJM: Whatever you say, *Mr. President*.

Imagine also in this regard the following hypothetical situation, ponders law professor Roseanna Sommers, in which

> Frank and Ellen meet at a night course and end up getting drinks together after class several times. The drinks start to feel like dates, so Ellen asks Frank if he is married, making it clear that adultery [would be] a deal-breaker for her. Frank *is* married [yet] lies and says he is single. The two go to bed. Is Frank guilty of rape?[1]

After all, she explains, "Ellen did not consent to have sex with a married man ... so the sex she had with Frank was not consensual."[2]

Indeed, consider the somewhat similar case of Sabbar Kashur, a Palestinian from East Jerusalem who was sentenced by an Israeli court to eighteen months in jail for having committed so-called rape by deception:

> Two years ago Kashur met a Jewish woman on the street in Jerusalem. He worked as a messenger for an Israeli law firm and like some other Palestinians looking to integrate more effectively into Israeli society had assumed the identity of a Jew. He called himself Dudu, a common Israeli name. On the same day the two had a consensual sexual encounter in a nearby office building. The woman ... did not know Kashur was an Arab. When she found out she filed a complaint with police. Kashur ... spent two years under house arrest facing a charge of rape and sexual assault. It was later dropped to the one of "rape by deception" in a plea bargain. In his verdict Judge Zvi Segal wrote "If she hadn't thought the accused was a Jewish bachelor ... she would not have cooperated."[3]

The profound socio-semiotic contrast between the *personal* and *social* identities respectively attached to the designations "Ashwin" and "Sir," "Andy" and "Mr. President," "Frank" and "a married man," and "Dudu" and "a Jewish bachelor" underscores a fundamental distinction between two contrasting visions of personhood—*personalness* and *impersonality*. And when Ratna finally utters Ashwin's name, it basically marks the symbolic transformation of an essentially "impersonal" relationship between two unspecified and thereby *generic* individuals (an "employer" and an "employee") into an effectively "personal" relationship between two *specific* ones ("Ashwin" and "Ratna").

The tremendous tension between the mental acts of envisioning (and thereby relating to) people "personally" and "impersonally" is indeed the main theme of Cy Crane and Herbert Weiner's aptly titled Platters song "I'm Just a Dancing Partner," which opens with the following set of identity-probing questions:

> Am I *just another dancing partner*?
> Do you smile at *every boy* this way?
> Do you hold them *all* until they're breathless?
> Do you *always* find nice things to say?
> When this dance is over, will you dance with *me* once more?

The fundamental contrast between the designations "me" and "just another dancing partner" (as well as "every boy" or for that matter "all"), of course, is essentially one between personalness and impersonality. And whereas the former effectively relates to specific individuals ("Ashwin," "Andy," "Frank," "Dudu," "me") distinctly characterized by their *singularity*, the latter views them as members of certain generic categories (an "employer," a "president," a "married man," a "Jewish bachelor," "just another dancing partner"). Rather than focusing on their specificity in an effort to capture "*who*" they are ("Romeo," "Juliet"), it thus foregrounds their genericity, effectively featuring "*what*" they are ("a Montague," "a Capulet").

Specific ("Who") Personhood

In marked contrast to impersonality, personalness features *particular* individuals, effectively characterized by their *distinctiveness* and therefore *idiosyncrasies*. In other words, it involves an essentially *personcentric* vision of people (and as evidenced by the considerable

4 DON'T TAKE IT PERSONALLY

semiotic contrast between the designations "a dog" and "Rover," as well as of our pets) that highlights their singularity as *unique* individuals, as officially emblematized by their pronouncedly distinctive personal signature, Social Security number, account user ID and password, and fingerprints. Such vision of personhood also underlies the notion of individuals' distinctive personal "style"—as evidenced, for example, in art (Frédéric Chopin, Jackson Pollock, Ingmar Bergman), haute cuisine,[4] sport (Muhammad Ali, Nadia Comăneci, Lionel Messi), as well as humor (Woody Allen, Bill Maher, Stephen Colbert)—or, for that matter, "sound" (Billie Holiday, Paul Desmond, Édith Piaf).

Essentially envisioning the individual as effectively detachable from any social group or community of which he or she is a member,[5] personalness has also given rise to ultimately personcentric literary genres such as the diary, the memoir, the biography, and the novel, which basically feature specific individuals. In stark contrast to epic poems and allegorical tales, for example, the novel, argues Ian Watt, is distinctly characterized by its pronounced effort to *singularize* its characters as "completely individualised entities"[6] instead of as *unspecified* human "types." Consider, for instance, in this regard the way Emma describes her husband Charles in Gustave Flaubert's *Madame Bovary*: "As he grew older his manner grew heavier . . . after eating he cleaned his teeth with his tongue; in taking soup he made a gurgling noise with every spoonful."[7] Such ultimately idiosyncratic details are highly *particularized* and, as such, distinctly characteristic of the novel as an artistic genre.[8] Can one even imagine using such details in characterizing effectively *archetypal* (and thereby unmistakably impersonalized) mythical figures such as Shiva, Elijah, Prometheus, or Quetzalcoatl?

As exemplified, for instance, by Stefan Zweig's novella *Letter from an Unknown Woman* as well as Paul McCartney's song "Michelle," personalness also underlies our romantic notion of love. Like Ashwin and Ratna's cross-class romance, Edward VIII's willingness to abdicate the British throne in order to be able to marry two-time divorcée Wallis Simpson ("the woman I love") perfectly emblematizes lovers' defiance of effectively impersonal interpersonal barriers. William Shakespeare's *Romeo and Juliet* and Garry Marshall and J. F. Lawton's *Pretty Woman*

"WHO" VERSUS "WHAT" 5

are some classic manifestations of such pronouncedly personcentric sentiment.

By the same token, in essentially foregrounding friends' distinctiveness (as when choosing with whom to share one's intimate personal information, or trying to anticipate on whose help one can count in moments of need), friendship perfectly exemplifies such vision of personhood. Friends, after all, are distinctly characterized by their singularity as "special" (and, as such, ultimately specific) individuals.

Personalness, of course, also underlies our effectively singularized notions of both "celebrity" and "charisma." The latter's original Christian characterization of an individual as having been personally endowed with the grace of God was famously extended by Max Weber to spiritual leadership in general, and thus to both Christian (Jesus, Joseph Smith, Billy Graham) and other (Muhammad, the Ba'al Shem Tov, Maharishi Mahesh Yogi) religious leaders. In fact, it was also extended by Weber to political as well as military leadership,[9] thereby also being attributed to individuals such as Julius Caesar, Napoleon Bonaparte, Winston Churchill, and Mahatma Gandhi, and has since been even further popularly extrapolated to the domains of art (Pablo Picasso, Salvador Dalí), music (Franz Liszt, Elvis Presley), film (James Dean, Greta Garbo), sport (Michael Jordan, Usain Bolt), as well as science (Albert Einstein, Stephen Hawking).[10]

Charisma is ultimately characterized by its association with specific individuals' alleged *extraordinariness*. A "charismatic" leader's qualities thus include pronouncedly *exceptional* skills such as the ability to inspire people, predict the future, and/or heal. What characterizes allegedly "charismatic" figures, in short, is their perceived image as *atypical*, their being "considered extraordinary and treated as endowed with . . . specifically exceptional powers or qualities."[11] Such individuals are thereby specifically characterized as antithetical to whatever we conventionally consider ordinary.

In stark contrast to other forms of authority based, for example, on formal rules and abstract principles,[12] *charismatic authority*, as famously identified by Weber,[13] is thus associated with the allegedly unique and thereby distinctive qualities of the specific individuals to whom the charisma is singularly attributed. Such authority, in other words, is thus based on those particular individuals' alleged "personal

6 DON'T TAKE IT PERSONALLY

qualities"[14] as specific persons and, as such, is grounded in a pronouncedly personcentric vision of personhood. It would therefore be utterly inconceivable, for example, to envision Benito Mussolini applying for an ultimately generic position of *a* (rather than *the*) duce, or, for that matter, Abraham for a position of *a* (instead of *the*) founder of monotheism.

In his presidential nomination acceptance speech at the 2016 Republican National Convention, then-candidate Donald Trump told prospective voters: "Nobody knows the system better than me, which is why *I alone* can fix it."[15] That pronouncement, so prophetically emblematic of Trump's presidential as well as post-presidential vision of utterly personalized politics (in marked contrast to the notion of voting, for example, for "*a* Democrat" or "*a* Republican" instead of for a specific person), succinctly captures the essence of charismatic authority, effectively foreshadowing his later reputation as "a different kind of," "not an ordinary" president.[16] Indeed, as Air Force One lifted off the runway four and a half years later carrying him on his final trip as a sitting president hours before the inauguration of his successor, Joe Biden, his pronouncedly defiant parting message beaming from the loudspeakers was, quite characteristically, Frank Sinatra's rendition of "My Way," Paul Anka's famous tribute to personal distinctiveness:

> For what is a man, what has he got?
> If not himself, then he has naught
> To say the things he truly feels
> And not the words of one who kneels
> The record shows I took the blows
> And did it *my* way[17]

Attributing charisma, continues Weber, usually implies a "complete personal devotion" to its alleged possessor,[18] and during the final months of Trump's presidency, let alone his early post-presidency, America's Republican Party indeed chose to follow the path of personal loyalty over that of ultimately impersonal policy[19] by establishing a so-called cult of personality, the modern political form of charismatic authority[20] so famously exemplified by Adolf Hitler in Germany, Joseph Stalin in the Soviet Union, Mao Zedong in China, Kim Il-sung in North Korea, Enver Hoxha in Albania, Juan Perón in Argentina, Nicolae Ceaușescu in Romania, Saddam Hussein in Iraq, Saparmurat Niyazov in Turkmenistan, Hugo Chávez in Venezuela, and Robert Mugabe in Zimbabwe. It thus came as no surprise when in summer 2021 Trump's "Save America" political action committee in fact urged his supporters to start carrying a red-and-gold embossed "Official Trump Card" plastic badge as a public display of their total personal loyalty to him.[21]

Generic ("What") Personhood

In sharp contrast to personalness, which highlights individuals' specificity, impersonality involves foregrounding their genericity. As exemplified by contrasting the ultimately impersonal act of disclosing sensitive financial information about oneself to the Internal Revenue Service agent who happens to process one's tax returns or making a confession to an effectively generic police investigator, for instance, to that of confiding in a specific close friend, it basically involves envisioning as well as relating to people "in a way that *does not depend on their personal identity.*"[22]

Consider, for example, a situation in which a company representative asks a customer to provide identification documentation. Rather than being an instance of one specific individual personally distrusting another, it actually constitutes a routine, pronouncedly impersonal request made by an essentially generic "company representative" (an "*imperson,*" so to speak) from an equally generic "customer" (yet another "imperson") regardless of the specific personal identities of the particular individual incumbents of those two social "roles." As such, it would therefore also be made by *any other* company representative from *any other* customer in a similar situation.

That explains the common use of the effectively impersonal expression "*It's nothing personal*" (or, for that matter, "*Don't take it personally*; he does that to *everyone*"). In other words, so goes the argument, "Don't take it personally: Work out what is *specifically* about you and what is a *general* complaint that you happen to get. . . . When it's not *specific* to you, don't take it as if it was."[23]

8 DON'T TAKE IT PERSONALLY

Such pronouncedly *non-personcentric* and therefore impersonal social logic also underlies the way the laws governing the relations between "landlords" and their "tenants" or "employers" and their "employees," or for that matter traffic rules, are typically articulated, so that if two cars arrive at an intersection at the same time, for example, the right-of-way goes to "the car on the right," regardless of its driver's personal identity. Rather than going to a specific individual, in other words, it actually goes to *anyone* who happens to be on the right, *no matter who* he or she is. In stark contrast to specific "someoneness,"[24] such generic "*anyoneness*,"[25] indeed, is what impersonality basically implies.

Consider also the way people nowadays screen potential romantic partners in online dating (or used to do in pre-digital newspaper purportedly "personal" ads), where ultimately specific individuals are nevertheless often featured and thereby envisioned generically in terms of their race, sexual orientation, occupation, or general political bent, for instance. Like recruiters screening job applicants' résumés, dating apps thus effectively transform particular individuals' supposedly "personal" characteristics into ultimately generic components of by-and-large impersonal so-called profiles.

Indeed, there is an ultimately impersonal dimension to the way we have always been choosing our romantic partners. After all, even modern Western non-arranged choices that may appear strictly personcentric (and, as such, "personal") nevertheless involve tacit impersonal considerations based, for example, on gender, age, ethnicity, religion, and social class. This is quite evident in the case of both the generic categories people prefer ("tall," "college-educated," "living in the Boston metropolitan area") and those they either explicitly or at least implicitly avoid (such as same-sex, interracial, or ones involving excessive genealogical proximity). We thus tacitly refrain from even considering members of certain social categories (parents, siblings, other "close relatives") as potential romantic partners, effectively regarding them as erotically irrelevant.[26] And given the conventional tacit norm of "compulsory heterosexuality,"[27] despite the fact that I never consciously confined my romantic choices to female potential partners, I likewise always tacitly assumed that, being a man, those were indeed my only options.

"WHO" VERSUS "WHAT"   9

Consider also in this regard the effectively generic commitment then-candidate Biden made in 2020 to appoint "a Black woman" (that is, "what") to the United States Supreme Court if he were in fact to become president two years before his pronouncedly personcentric official decision to nominate Ketanji Brown Jackson (that is, specifically "who") for that job. Indeed, as evidenced by comparing the set of characters listed on the first page of a playscript to the eventual list of the cast members printed in the play's theatrical program (or, for that matter, a preliminary discussion of a department's hiring needs when drafting an academic job advertisement, as articulated in such terms as "an environmental sociologist" or "a criminologist," to the eventual discussion of the actual candidates), even when people are ultimately related to as specific individuals, they are often initially envisioned in terms of their effectively generic social "roles." By the same token, even though in the late-2020 COVID-19 vaccine rollouts it was ultimately specific individuals who actually got vaccinated, they were nevertheless in fact initially viewed as members of unmistakably generic categories such as "elderly people with underlying conditions" or "first responders." *Relating to individuals in terms of specifically "who" they are is thus often preceded by envisioning them in terms of generically "what" they are.*

Furthermore, as so evocatively captured by Emile Durkheim's notion of *"homo duplex,"*[28] every individual is actually envisioned by others as a combination of *both* personal and impersonal elements of personhood and can therefore in fact be related to personally as well as impersonally. The tremendous symbolic significance of switching from "Sir" (that is, generically "what") to "Ashwin" (that is, specifically "who") notwithstanding, even proper names are only rarely strictly singular, indeed constituting a combination of *personal as well as ultimately impersonal* (gender, ethnic, generational) identifying elements,[29] thereby reminding us that, as effectively complementary visions of personhood, personalness and impersonality are by no means mutually exclusive.

In fact, personalness and impersonality are but the "ideal-typical"[30] opposite poles of a spectrum actually featuring many combinations of the two, as exemplified, for instance, by pronouncedly ritualized (and, as such, highly scripted) yet nonetheless personcentric social occasions

10   DON'T TAKE IT PERSONALLY

ranging from courtroom trials and award ceremonies to birthday parties, weddings, as well as funerals. Therefore, although I purposefully exaggerate the conceptual contrast between them for analytical reasons, they are effectively relational terms ultimately referring only to *more* personal and *more* impersonal visions of personhood.

And indeed, just like the somewhat parallel distinction between "intimate" and "impersonal" social ties,[31] the one between our specific and generic visions of personhood is by no means strictly binary. Lest one forget, therefore, the mutual separateness of personalness and impersonality is actually analytical rather than empirical. In the real world, after all, as if mirroring the somewhat parallel relation between speech and language,[32] the "personal" and the "impersonal" are in fact entangled in each other as two effectively complementary visions of personhood, the relative proportions between which vary historically, cross-culturally, as well as across different social situations.

Sociology and Impersonality

The distinction between personalness and impersonality implies our ability to epistemically *transcend individuals' singularity* and also view them generically. As such, it allows us to envision relations not only between specific individuals but also between an "uncle" and a "nephew," a "plaintiff" and a "defendant," a "buyer" and a "seller," and a "student" and a "teacher."

Such epistemic ability characterizes humans in general but particularly sociologists. Indeed, it constitutes one of the fundamental pillars of the distinctly *sociological* perspective sometimes referred to as "the sociological imagination" thereby effectively providing "a way of understanding what sociology is all about."[33] As Lewis Coser so succinctly summed up the essence of thinking distinctly sociologically, "The sociologist is concerned with *King* John, not with King *John*"[34]— that is, not with specific individuals but, rather, with the ultimately generic social *positions* they occupy.

And yet to date, no sociologist has ever comprehensively theorized the intricate relations between our specific and generic visions of

"WHO" VERSUS "WHAT" 11

personhood. As a result, even the fundamental constitutive elements of impersonality have yet to be explicitly articulated.

Indeed, not coincidentally, it is precisely because of its centrality to the distinctive way sociologists think that impersonality has thus far been professionally taken for granted, thereby remaining figuratively hidden in plain sight.[35] And as such, it has therefore never been considered yet a social phenomenon worth exploring in its own right rather than as but an aspect of marketization and bureaucratization, such as for Weber, or commodification and urbanization, such as for Georg Simmel. As a result, despite the fact that every sociologist is most likely at least implicitly cognizant of the fundamental tension between personalness and impersonality, it has yet to be explicitly theorized. And that, indeed, is what I try to do in this book.

2

"Who" Versus "How Many"

> The life of women in the corporation was influenced by the proportions in which they found themselves. . . . It was rarity and scarcity, rather than femaleness *per se*, that shaped the environment for women in the parts of [the corporation] mostly populated by men.
>
> —Rosabeth M. Kanter
> *Men and Women of the Corporation*, 207

Social Arithmetic

When our daughter was little, she used to distinguish seemingly simple "one-parent decisions," as she quite resourcefully used to call them, from what appeared to be more complex "two-parent" ones, *regardless of which particular parent* she would need to ask his or her permission to do something.

The profound contrast between "*who-*" and "*what-*based" ways of envisioning people certainly captures the fundamental tension between our personal and impersonal visions of personhood, yet not as compellingly as the even more profound contrast between "who-" and "*how-many-*based" social cognition. Although deciding which particular individual (that is, specifically "who") I choose to be my tango partner is implicitly preceded by deciding that, since I am a man, it would most likely be a woman (that is, generically "what"), even that decision is nevertheless not quite as impersonal as my tacit prior decision that I would actually choose *one* person (that is, generically "how many"). After all, as the saying goes, it takes two to tango.

The actual sequential order in which we make such decisions reveals their ultimately *arithmetical* underpinnings, as likewise exemplified by

Don't Take It Personally. Eviatar Zerubavel, Oxford University Press. © Eviatar Zerubavel 2024.
DOI: 10.1093/oso/9780197691335.003.0002

the fact that deciding to declare three (gold, silver, and bronze) medal winners, for instance, tacitly precedes the decision as to which specific individuals would actually be awarded those medals. By the same token, a company's effectively impersonal decision to lay off twenty of its employees and only later determine specifically who those twenty would in fact be is fundamentally different from one specifically targeting those particular individuals from the start. Indeed, the public debate whether former Federal Bureau of Investigation Director James Comey's and Deputy Director Andrew McCabe's Internal Revenue Service audits were purely coincidental or politically motivated[1] revolved entirely around whether selecting them for those exceptionally unusual audits was done randomly (and, as such, impersonally) or whether they were specifically (and thereby personally) literally "singled" out.

The expression "it takes two to tango" exemplifies the pronouncedly impersonal social logic underlying numerically designated collective entities (a string "quartet," a typically twelve-person jury) that are effectively independent of their actual individual constituents, whom we socially envision not only as specific persons but also as generic "impersons." The unmistakably impersonal character of such entities—in other words, the fact that their "form no longer depends upon any contents of [their] component individuals," as Simmel so brilliantly observed—is indeed "nowhere seen in a more absolute and emphatic manner than in the reduction of the principles of [social] organization to purely *arithmetic* relations."[2] Such fundamentally *arithmetical vision of personhood* thus involves "a diminution of the specific . . . content of the individual personality and its substitution by the formal fact that the perso[n] is, simply, *one*"![3] Its most distinctive manifestation, in short, is the fact that an individual's who-based personal identity is considered of only secondary significance to his or her how-many-based social identity as a member of a particular group or category of people conventionally designated in terms of a specified number of ultimately generic and thereby impersonal structural "*slots*" (a six-person volleyball team, the nine-person United States Supreme Court).

And indeed, as so explicitly exemplified by the so-called *head counts* conducted by congressional whips prior to a major vote as well

14 DON'T TAKE IT PERSONALLY

as by tour leaders before proceeding from one site on their itinerary to the next, we are basically dealing here with a pronouncedly *quantitative* view of personhood that fundamentally rejects the effectively personcentric attention to individuals' idiosyncratic (and, as such, distinctive) "qualities." In other words, it is a way of *envisioning actual persons as sheer quantities "without regard for the peculiarities of the individuals* who constitute those numbers."[4]

The profound contrast between our quantitative (and, as such, impersonal) and "qualitative" (and, as such, personal) visions of personhood[5] ultimately boils down to the fundamental difference between *counting* and "weighing,"[6] a sociomental process effectively highlighting "qualitative" differences even between arithmetically identical entities[7] (such as all-male and all-female five-person basketball teams, for instance). And perhaps nowhere is the tension between the two more chillingly portrayed than in William Styron's aptly titled novel *Sophie's Choice*, where a Josef Mengele-like Nazi doctor offers a mother the horrifying choice of deciding which *one* of her two children will be given the opportunity to maybe survive Auschwitz and which one would most certainly end her short life there.[8]

Such a pronouncedly arithmetical vision of personhood is also evidenced in the way we view people *statistically*, as manifested, for example, in the manner we usually calculate risk (as in "one in a hundred-thousand chance"), or in how we often think about war casualties as well as victims of natural disasters. And when social scientists, pollsters, and psychologists conduct their surveys, interviews, opinion polls, and experiments, they too typically disregard the distinctive personal idiosyncrasies of the specific individuals they study or poll, instead focusing on their ultimately impersonal *quantity*, such as when deciding in advance *how many* people (rather than specifically who) they should survey, interview, poll, or include in their experiment.

Indeed, such an effectively arithmetical vision of personhood also underlies predominantly statistically based sciences such as demography and epidemiology. After all, as they examine crime, fertility, housing, or even suicide or divorce statistics, for instance, demographers in fact look at entire populations rather than at their non-aggregated, specific individual constituents.[9] By the same token, as they count the numbers of fatally infected, hospitalized, as well as,

"WHO" VERSUS "HOW MANY" 15

for that matter, vaccinated persons during pandemics, epidemiologists also focus on *aggregate numbers of cases* rather than on specific individuals. Indeed, the profound contrast between the news stories featuring the specific casualties of the COVID-19 pandemic and the statistical analyses surrounding their aggregate numbers perfectly exemplified the fundamental tension between our personal and impersonal visions of personhood.

Quotas

An ultimately arithmetical vision of personhood is also evidenced in the form of *quotas*, effectively articulated in such terms as "*no less than*" or "*no more than*" a specified number of individuals.

Some quotas, for instance, are thus defined in terms of *a minimum number of persons required*, as when at least a certain number of students need to preregister in order for a particular workshop or seminar to actually be offered. Such quotas are likewise evidenced in situations in which at least a certain number of signatories is required for nominating somebody for a particular position or putting a particular proposition on the ballot, as well as in affirmative-action initiatives, such as when a company is expected to hire *at least a certain percentage* of members of traditionally underrepresented categories of employees (women, African Americans) in an effort to increase its social diversity.

Consider also the *quorum*, the minimum number of persons required to sign off on a dissertation, for instance, or hold a vote to change an organization's bylaws. A classic example of a quorum is the *minyan*, the ten-person minimum required by Jewish law in order to conduct a communal worship gathering, and the Yiddish proverb "Nine rabbis can't make a minyan, but ten cobblers can"[10] perfectly captures the socio-arithmetical spirit of privileging quantity over "quality."

The exact reverse logic underlies the diametrically opposite socio-arithmetical practice of setting *a maximum number of persons allowed*, as evidenced, for instance, in the official restrictions on the number of persons (typically articulated in terms of specified percentages of full capacity) that were allowed to eat at the same time in a given restaurant

16 DON'T TAKE IT PERSONALLY

during the COVID-19 pandemic, or on the number of people allowed to enter a given movie theater due to fire regulations or go on a particularly dangerous amusement-park ride. It is also exemplified by the equivalent practice of "capping" the number of students allowed to enroll in special honors courses.

Such socio-arithmetical logic has likewise manifested itself in emergency regulations limiting the number of individuals allowed to gather outdoors outside curfew hours, in the *numerus clausus* (the Latin for "closed numbers") restrictions on the number of Jews permitted to attend various European universities as well as enter certain professions in the 1930s, and in draconian immigration policies like the one implemented by the 1924 Immigration Act, which effectively restricted the number of immigrants from certain countries allowed to enter the United States every year. It infamously also allowed the Nazis to systematically project how many thousands of concentration camp inmates they would be able to exterminate every day based on the *maximum "processing" capacity* of their trains, gas chambers, cleaning crews, and crematoria—a horrifically vivid testament to the pronouncedly impersonal character of the bureaucratic imagination.[11]

Political Arithmetic

The way we *envision individuals as countable quantities* is also captured by the term *per capita* (the Latin for "for each head"), which, given that people each have exactly one head, tacitly underscores the fact that we usually count each individual as exactly one, as so perfectly exemplified by the way bus, subway, railroad, and airline companies normally charge passengers *per person*, regardless of the actual amount of seat space their body in fact occupies relative to other passengers. And even when some airlines do establish a special "overweight passengers policy," they actually require passengers "who are unable to secure their seatbelt, who are unable to lower the armrests, and who are encroaching too much on the personal space of the person sitting next to them" to purchase two tickets,[12] thereby still applying an arithmetically standardized (and, as such, pronouncedly impersonal) vision of personhood.

"WHO" VERSUS "HOW MANY"   17

Envisioning people as countable quantities does not necessarily also imply, however, viewing each particular individual as simply one. Thus, for example, at the 1787 U.S. Constitutional Convention, as a political compromise that would allow states to increase the number of their electoral votes without also having to put free persons and slaves on an equal footing and regard them as political equals, each state was allowed to also include three-fifths of its slave population (that is, to effectively count every five slaves as three free persons) in determining its formal representation in Congress, thereby tacitly implying viewing slaves as constituting only three-fifths of full-fledged persons!

If this unabashedly racist so-called Three-Fifths Compromise strikes many of us today as particularly offensive, it is because it obviously violated the spirit of the pronouncedly *egalitarian* notion famously articulated by Thomas Jefferson in the preamble to the U.S. Declaration of Independence that "All men are created equal." Drawing on the ultimately arithmetical definition of equality ("the quality of being the same in quantity"),[13] the idea that *all individuals are considered arithmetically equal*[14] in fact constitutes a fundamental pillar of our vision of democracy.

Effectively applying the pronouncedly impersonal arithmetico-political logic of egalitarianism, democracy is philosophically grounded in a strictly quantitative vision of personhood that involves simply counting people's votes, for example, as Simmel so astutely observed, rather than qualitatively "weighing" them.[15] In other words, it "assigns the same symbolic weight to each individual," thereby considering all group members arithmetically equal components of the group.[16] Reginald Rose's depiction of the distinctly democratic process of jury deliberation in the American courtroom drama *Twelve Angry Men* offers a classic portrayal of such process of political "leveling."

In democracy, in short, each person's vote is considered effectively equivalent to anyone else's, thereby exemplifying the quintessentially egalitarian political principle of "One Person, One Vote." One thus loses a vote only when the number of individuals objecting to one's proposition exceeds the number of those who support it (that is, when one is literally "outvoted"). Democracy, in other words, promotes the *majority rule*, the pronouncedly impersonal arithmetico-political

18 DON'T TAKE IT PERSONALLY

logic according to which "the numerical majority of a population [has] the final say in determining the outcome of a decision."[17] Yet *majoritarianism* has also had its share of critics, some of whom have even gone as far as using the expression "*tyranny of the majority*"[18] to characterize the tremendous danger posed by rendering the opinions of members of numerical minorities politically irrelevant, as so famously exemplified by John Stuart Mill's impassioned libertarian call to protect the rights of what is ultimately the most vulnerable form of such a minority—the individual:

> Protection . . . against the tyranny of the magistrate is not enough; there needs protection also against *the tyranny of the prevailing opinion* and feeling, against the tendency of society to impose . . . its own ideas and practices as rules of conduct on those who dissent from them; to fetter the development and, if possible, *prevent the formation of any individuality* not in harmony with its ways, and compel all characters to fashion themselves upon the model of its own.[19]

Furthermore, ever since Aristotle first contrasted the principles of establishing equality "on the basis of number" and "on the basis of merit,"[20] the majority rule has in fact been challenged not only by those who wish to protect individuality but also by those who champion aristocracy (the Greek for "the rule of the best") over democracy (the Greek for "the rule of the people"). The very notion of preferring how-many- to what-based decisions thus offends their ultimately elitist sensibility, which favors considerations of "quality" over those of sheer quantity, leading them to protest relegating the former to political irrelevance.

That explains their vigorous opposition to the quintessentially democratic notion that winning is a strictly arithmetical matter, and that losing a vote is therefore not a result of being wrong but of being in the minority. Such deep antipathy toward "the omnipotence of the majority"[21] has been perhaps most compellingly articulated by Alexis de Tocqueville, for whom "the moral authority of the majority is . . . based upon the notion . . . that the *number*" of those who vote "is more important than their *quality*,"[22] as well as by Simmel, for whom the very notion "that an opinion, only because its exponents are more numerous

"WHO" VERSUS "HOW MANY" 19

than those of another opinion," should be regarded as the opinion of the entire group is "an entirely undemonstrable dogma."[23]

And indeed, despite the current politico-cultural predominance of the distinctly democratic principle whereby "everyone counts as one and no one counts for more than one"[24] (as evidenced, for instance, even by the common practice of counting "likes" as well as the number of one's "followers" on social media),

> to subject the individual to majority decision through the fact that others—not superior, but equal—hold a different opinion is not as natural as it may appear to us today. It is unknown in ancient German law, which states that whoever does not agree with the decision of the community is not bound by it; outvoting did not exist in the tribal council of the Iroquois, in the Cortes of Aragon up to the sixteenth century, or in the parliament of Poland. . . . Decisions that were not unanimous were not valid.[25]

In other words, the notion that the minority must conform to the majority, such that the "qualitative value of the individual voice" is thereby effectively "reduced to an entity of purely quantitative significance,"[26] is but a social convention.

Social Fractions

As so explicitly evidenced by the infamous "Three-Fifths Compromise," the "arithmetized" individual is socially envisioned not only as an integer ("one") but also as a fraction (*"one of . . ."*)—a *social fraction*, so to speak—that is, as one of 388 signatories to a particular petition, a member of a "party of four" who made a dinner reservation for 7:30 p.m., or someone's generically designated "plus one" or "and guest" (that is, one of a party of two) at a wedding. As part of a numerically designated collective entity, one's "character as a group member has completely superseded its individual and differentiated character."[27]

Such supersession is explicitly exemplified, for instance, by the socio-mnemonic practice aptly dubbed by Yael Zerubavel "numerical

20   DON'T TAKE IT PERSONALLY

commemoration,"[28] whereby certain historical figures are in fact collectively remembered not so much as specific individuals but as integral parts of numerically designated groups, such as in the cases of the Israeli city of Kiryat Shmona (the Hebrew for "The City of the Eight")[29] or the so-called Thirty-Three Orientals nationally commemorated on Uruguay's "Landing of the 33 Patriots Day." And although only few Christians today may actually remember Melchior, Balthasar, or Gaspar as individuals, they are nevertheless collectively (and thereby impersonally) remembered as "The Three Wise Men."

Furthermore, the very notion of a "social fraction" also underscores the sociological significance of relative *proportions* rather than just absolute numbers,[30] which helps explain, for instance, why the extent to which a person tends to attract more attention or be more commonly stereotyped may be partly a function of whether he or she is *one of many* or *one of just a few* (thereby constituting a plurality, let alone a majority, or a numerical minority, respectively).[31] "The life of women in the corporation," for example, observes Rosabeth Kanter, is thus

> influenced by the *proportions* in which they f[i]nd themselves. Those women who [a]re *few in number* among male peers and often ha[ve] "*only* woman" status bec[o]me tokens: symbols of how-women-can-do, stand-ins for all women.... At the same time, they also ech[o] the experiences of people of any kind who are *rare* and *scarce*: the *lone* black among whites, the *lone* man among women, the *few* foreigners among natives. Any situation where proportions of significant types of people are highly skewed can produce similar themes and processes. It [i]s *rarity* and *scarcity*, rather than femaleness per se, that shap[e] the environment for women in the parts of [the corporation] mostly populated by men.[32]

Needless to say, as evidenced by the difference in how we respond to the news that eight-hundred-thousand people died of famine this year and to a story about one particular child who is dying from starvation, the impersonal vision of personhood tends to become more pronounced as the number of individuals constituting a social fraction's denominator increases (that is, as their relative proportion decreases). One of the most distinctive features of two-person relations compared

"WHO" VERSUS "HOW MANY" 21

to two-hundred- (let alone two-thousand-person) ones, after all, is the fact that each of the individuals involved in the latter tends to be far less noticeable, let alone singularly identifiable. That explains, for instance, the considerable difference in the amount of pronouncedly personcentric social pressure one might experience to demonstrate one's personal commitment to relationships in which one is one of just a few compared to ones of being one of many, as exemplified by the fundamental difference in the level of urgency one feels to respond to an email sent only to oneself and to an eighty-six-person listserv. By the same token, having noticed students occasionally dozing off in a class of forty people yet never in one of only five makes me fully cognizant of the social arithmetic of personalness and impersonality!

3

The Anatomy of Impersonality

> When the unique person of the other disappears behind the *type*, and alter is reduced in ego's perception to an instance of some general *category*, we may say that the relationship has become impersonal.
>
> —Renate Mayntz, "The Nature and Genesis of Impersonality," 428. Emphases added

To fully capture the essence of impersonality, we first need to examine its fundamental constitutive elements, namely (a) social identity, (b) typicality, (c) standardness, and (d) substitutability. Those, indeed, are the four main ingredients constituting the kind of social interactions and relations we consider "impersonal."

Social Identity

There is a fundamental sociological distinction between a person who occasionally smokes a cigarette, which we conventionally regard as something that she merely "does," and someone to whom we in fact attach the *identity* (or "*persona*") of "a smoker," which we conventionally regard as what she actually "is."[1] We likewise distinguish the fleeting verb-like quality of describing someone as having "*drunk* his wine in three gulps" from actually characterizing him with the noun-like supposed essence of being "a heavy *drinker*," let alone "a drunk," which, in marked contrast to the former description, we indeed consider identity-salient.[2]

Furthermore, as we have seen, the distinction between personalness and impersonality presupposes an additional distinction between

Don't Take It Personally. Eviatar Zerubavel, Oxford University Press. © Eviatar Zerubavel 2024.
DOI: 10.1093/oso/9780197691335.003.0003

THE ANATOMY OF IMPERSONALITY   23

what Erving Goffman famously dubbed *"personal identity"* and *"social identity"*[3]—that is, between one's envisioned identity as a specific individual (such as "Frank," "Dudu," or "me") and "as a social being"[4] (such as "a married man," "a Jewish bachelor," or "a dancing partner"). And whereas highly personalized (and, as such, pronouncedly distinctive) birth certificates, passports, driver licenses, employee IDs, signatures, personal passwords, and biometric identifiers (facial and dental features, voice and retinal blood-vessel patterns, fingerprints) convey our envisioned singularity as specific, unique individuals,[5] the adjective "*a*" conveys our generic (and, as such, ultimately impersonal) characteristics. We thus have "a truck driver," "a school principal," and "a secretary," yet not "a Serena Williams," "a Sonny Rollins," or "a Robert Redford."

Thus, for example, at the universities where I used to teach, whereas referring to me as "Eviatar Zerubavel" captured my distinctly personal identity as a specific, singular individual, envisioning me as a "professor" underscored my pronouncedly generic social identity as a faculty member. And as implied by the use of the preposition "*as*" or "*qua*," while we conventionally have only one personal identity,[6] we each have multiple social identities. In different social contexts I can thus be identified as a "husband," a "father," a "scholar," a "mentor," a "friend," an "Israeli-born," a "baby boomer," a "film buff," a "track fan," and so on almost indefinitely.

By the same token, when interacting with a flight attendant, a lifeguard, or a bank teller, for instance, I am actually relating to them *not as specific individuals* but, rather, as a "flight attendant," "lifeguard," or "bank teller." And so is the way I think about my "accountant," my "plumber," my manuscript's "copy editor," or my "dentist."

The distinction between individuals' personal and social identities is manifested perhaps most dramatically when people explicitly try to separate their public persona from what they consider to be their actual, "true" self, effectively implying that what they "*do*" as school disciplinarians or janitors, for instance, does not exhaust, and may in fact even conflict with, who they believe they "*are*" as individuals.[7] It is also particularly pronounced in situations in which one's social identity is conventionally regarded as having greater cultural salience than one's personal identity to the point of actually overriding it, such as

24 DON'T TAKE IT PERSONALLY

in the case of socially marked and especially stigmatized identities. As satirically exemplified by the strikingly racialized adverbial expression "while Black" (as in Danny Pollard's book *Obama Guilty of Being President While Black*, for instance),[8] otherwise unmarked mundane activities such as jogging (as in Ahmaud Arbery's case) or even just simply walking (as in Trayvon Martin's case) might nevertheless be tragically enough criminalized when they are conducted "while being Black."[9]

On the other hand, however, an individual's social identity may actually be strategically invoked in an effort to effectively override his or her socially stigmatized (and, as such, "spoiled")[10] *personal* identity, as exemplified, for instance, by the Vatican's response to the protests against Pope John Paul II's 1987 official meeting with Austrian president Kurt Waldheim despite the latter's involvement in the deportations of thousands of Greek Jews to Nazi death camps in the 1940s. The Vatican's spokesman thus explicitly announced that "the Pope was welcoming Mr. Waldheim as the elected representative of the Austrian people and *not as an individual*."[11] A somewhat similar attempt to invoke one's social identity in an effort to draw public attention away from one's politically "damaged"[12] personal identity in the aftermath of the Watergate scandal was likewise made by President Richard Nixon in his 1974 resignation speech. Declaring that he had never been a quitter, Nixon said that to leave office before the official end of his term was "abhorrent to every instinct in my body. But *as President*, I must put the interests of America first."[13]

The notion of social identity presupposes a fundamental socioepistemic process aptly dubbed by Leon Festinger *de-individuation*, whereby people "do not pay attention to other individuals *qua* individuals" (and "correspondingly . . . do not feel they are singled out by others").[14] As such, it is often manifested in the form of what sociologists refer to as a social "*role*," a structural as well as functional position socially envisioned as distinct (and, as such, separate) from and therefore essentially independent of its specific occupants. Interactions between what would otherwise be considered specific individuals are thereby socially construed as ones between a "teacher" and a "student," a "doctor" and a "patient," or, for that matter, two "neighbors" or "co-workers." Such de-individuation is perfectly

THE ANATOMY OF IMPERSONALITY 25

exemplified by the ultimately impersonal spirit of the law, whereby pronouncedly generic and therefore impersonal social roles such as "plaintiff," "defendant," "judge," "juror," and "witness" are effectively viewed as transcending their specific incumbents so that a judge, for instance, is thus expected to "not ac[t] 'on his own,' but *qua judge*."[15]

Yet social identities also take the form of epistemic membership in certain social *categories*. We thus identify people not only as singular, specific individuals but also as members of particular categories[16] effectively articulated in pronouncedly impersonal terms of age, gender, race, ethnicity, religion, social class, sexual orientation, occupation, and even health status. As such, they are thus generically envisioned, for instance, as "middle-aged," "female," "white," "Lithuanian," "Christian," "middle-class," "bisexual," "musician," or "diabetic."

Furthermore, as pointed out by "social identity theorists" Henri Tajfel and John Turner,[17] such categories often take the form of social *groups*. As such, specific individuals are nevertheless often also socially identified and thereby envisioned in terms of their epistemic membership in a particular social "group" such as a nation, religious denomination, political party, generation, or profession, and thus, for example, as a "Tunisian," "Episcopalian," "Republican," "millennial," or "electrical engineer." In other words, whereas personalness implies highlighting people's specific, pronouncedly unique personal attributes and therefore singularity, impersonality often involves construing social identities based on their ultimately generic epistemic membership in particular social groups.

Lest one regard the distinction between personalness and impersonality as a binary one, and personcentric and "*group-centric*" identities as therefore mutually exclusive, however, consider not-so-clear-cut, effectively ambiguous situations such as getting an ostensibly personal letter that, as a member of an ultimately impersonal mailing list, I in fact receive as but one of hundreds of people, or watching by myself a television commercial that is nevertheless designed to also target millions of other viewers besides me. By the same token, when I watch the soccer World Cup, I am watching players who are actually identifiable *both* personally (by name as well as a distinctive jersey number) as specific individuals *and* impersonally (by a distinctive jersey color) as members of particular national "teams" (that is, as

26 DON'T TAKE IT PERSONALLY

"Italians," "Nigerians," or "Brazilians"). Such epistemic duality is even more pronounced when I listen to sports announcers commentating on a live international or intercollegiate (and, as such, effectively *"team-centric"*) relay race.

Typicality

Identifying people impersonally often involves viewing them as "representing" the social categories in which (or social "groups" to which) they epistemically "belong." Such *"epistemic representativeness"*[18] is particularly pronounced in the case of stigmatized social identities (such as being considered "transgender" or viewed as "disabled"), which, in sharp contrast to conventionally unmarked ones (such as "cisgender" or "able-bodied"), are often associated with particular, often negative cultural stereotypes. (We thus have abundant distinctive cultural stereotypes of "lesbians," "criminals," and "obsessive compulsives," for example, yet very few ones, if any, of straights, law-abiding citizens, or the so-called mentally healthy).[19] That is also true of other culturally marked social identities such as women, who are indeed often viewed *"as representatives of their category . . . rather than individuals."*[20] As late as the 1970s, for instance, women in the corporate world were thus "visible as *category members,* because of their social *type . . . representing their category, not just themselves."*[21]

As implied by such use of the term "type," epistemic representativeness presupposes the ultimately impersonal notion of *typicality.*[22] In sharp contrast to love, friendship, charisma, and other manifestations of personalness, which we conventionally associate with singularity and thus with *atypicality* ("the quality of not being representative of a type, group, or class"), identifying people in terms of their categorical or group epistemic membership involves a certain degree of perceived typicality. After all, "[our] tendency to generalize from the behavior of a specific group member to the group as a whole is proportional to [our] perception of the group's homogeneity,"[23] which presupposes typicality. A specific individual, in other words, can thus also be viewed as a "typical" (or "prototypical")[24] member (and, as such, an epistemic "representative") of conventional social categories such as

"Filipinos," "billionaires," or "vegetarians." Indeed, "when the unique person of the other disappears behind the type, and alter is reduced in ego's perception to an instance of some general category," we then "say that the relationship has become impersonal."[25] And the more we view people as supposedly typical "Southerners," "businessmen," or "liberals," for example, the more we tend to envision them as "social synecdoches,"[26] so to speak, epistemically "representing" the ultimately impersonal categories in which (or social groups to which) they purportedly "belong."

Standardness

In sharp contrast to the pronouncedly personcentric attribution of charisma, for example, which inevitably implies, as we shall see, considerable uncertainty, impersonality presumes a certain degree of predictability, as it involves certain typical *expectations* from "typical" members of particular social categories and groups as well as from "typical" occupants of particular social positions and incumbents of particular social roles. We thus expect specific individuals to nevertheless abide by ultimately impersonal rules of acceptable behavior *as* police officers, *as* therapists, *as* teachers, *as* coaches, or *as* priests. Furthermore, we expect them to do so in a pronouncedly *standard* (and, as such, effectively predictable) manner.

A critical implication of such emphasis on standardness is our expectation that, all other things being equal, every member of a given social category or group ("customer," "applicant," "student," "contestant," "defendant," "patient") would ultimately be granted *the same* treatment.[27] Such envisioned *uniformity* underlies, for example, the very idea of "the rule of law," which is why "Lady Justice" is indeed portrayed blindfolded, figuratively embodying the conventional expectation that laws would apply *equally* to *everyone* in an impartial and thus "blind" manner. Nothing, perhaps, captures the fundamental difference between personalness and impersonality more compellingly than the dramatic, irreconcilable contrast between Trump's persistent expectation to receive effectively personcentric (and, as such, preferential) legal treatment and the U.S. Department

28 DON'T TAKE IT PERSONALLY

of Justice's ultimately impersonal insistence that "No one," indeed, "is above the law."

By the same token, we also expect individual incumbents to nevertheless perform their social roles in a by-and-large uniform manner. That implies adhering to effectively impersonal *routine* (and, as such, standard) rules and procedures (that is, to certain "*protocols*"), which presupposes a fundamentally *formulaic* way[28] of conducting oneself in one's role.

Such standard routines, protocols, and formulas often take the form of literal as well as figurative *scripts*.[29] And indeed, as exemplified by both religious and national rituals such as reciting traditional wedding vows and the U.S. Pledge of Allegiance, scriptedness, which is the diametrical opposite of the ultimately personcentric act of *improvisation*, is one of the most common manifestations of standardness (and, thereby, impersonality):

> I . . . take you . . . to be my wife, to have and to hold from this day forward, for better or for worse, for richer or for poorer, in sickness and in health, I promise to love and cherish you.

> I pledge Allegiance to the flag of the United States of America, and to the Republic for which it stands, one nation under God, indivisible, with Liberty and Justice for all.

Consider also in this regard the pronouncedly scripted manner in which hospital staff sometimes provide patients with both legal and clinical information:

> I, *as a clinician, have to* give you this choice.

> There is something else I *have to* let you know.

> We *have to* give you some idea of the treatment you will be getting.

> These are Dr. ____'s initial findings. He *has to* tell you how he plans to treat you.[30]

THE ANATOMY OF IMPERSONALITY   29

As evidenced by contrasting, for instance, lovers' pronouncedly personcentric amorous discourse with such explicit use of the words "we," "have to," and "as a clinician," informing their patients is an ultimately scripted process that involves hospital staff's professional roles rather than their specific incumbents who actually provide such information.

Substitutability

Although "who" the specific incumbents of a given social role are ("Margaret," "Christopher") is effectively distinct from "what" they are ("a customer representative," "a supermarket cashier"), it sometimes may not actually matter that much anyway. Indeed, they are often viewed as but the temporary occupants of a given generic (and therefore impersonal) "slot in the social structure" and, as such, as also functionally *substitutable* with one another.[31] When having to deal with one of her aforementioned "one-parent decisions," for instance, our then-young daughter would in fact sometimes literally address my wife and me jointly as "Mommy or Daddy" rather than singularly as either distinctly "Mommy" or distinctly "Daddy." As implicitly exemplified by her remarkably casual use of the conjunction "*or,*" one of the most critical characteristics of impersonality, indeed, is our epistemic ability to view members of a given social category (such as "parent," in this case) generically, and thereby somewhat *interchangeably*, rather than just as singularly identifiable and therefore specifiable individuals.

Viewing people as effectively interchangeable with others is ultimately antithetical to relating to them as specific individuals. Their envisioned standardness (and, as such, "anyoneness") thus stands in diametrical opposition to the conventional envisioned singularity of friends, lovers, celebrities, and charismatic leaders. (Contrast, for example, the experiences of hearing Antonio Vivaldi or Niccolò Paganini in concert and being serenaded by a relatively unknown—and, as such, effectively substitutable—Gypsy violinist at some Hungarian restaurant.) The fundamental sociological contrast, as explicitly characterized by Simmel, is thus indeed between viewing them personally as specific,

30 DON'T TAKE IT PERSONALLY

"particular individuals" and impersonally as "any interchangeable person[s]."[32]

Such epistemic substitutability is evidenced, for example, in the *collective* sense of responsibility *jointly* shared by several group members (siblings, co-authors, business partners) together (that is, *as a group*) rather than as singular individuals.[33] And it is indeed the fact that she shares her professional responsibility for patients with other, functionally equivalent (and, as such, officially substitutable) "emergency room nurses," for instance, that ultimately makes it officially possible for *any* specific emergency room nurse to leave the hospital and go home at the end of her shift.[34]

Such substitutability is likewise exemplified by the practice of collective punishment, whereby people are essentially being punished not for their own wrongdoings as specific individuals (that is, personally) but, rather, for those committed by other fellow members of the social category in which (or social group to which) they epistemically "belong" (that is, impersonally). By the same token, it is also manifested in situations in which people returning from an "exotic" trip abroad stop at the airport gift shop to buy several pronouncedly "typical" (that is, supposedly "representative" and, as such, ultimately generic) souvenirs without assigning them in their head yet to their specific future recipients. And it also characterizes "small talk," where almost the exact same comments about the weather one makes in a conversation with one particular individual are also made in his or her conversations with others.[35]

An even more extreme manifestation of the mutual epistemic substitutability of the various members of a given social category or group is the tendency to view them as if they were actually nameless and thereby lacking any distinctive personal identity as specific individuals. As Simmel so succinctly characterized the relation between substitutability and *namelessness*, or *anonymity*, "the more anonymous" and therefore impersonally envisioned one is, indeed, "the more fit is he [sic] to step into the place of another."[36]

As evidenced by the use of *masks*, the most common corrective to the tremendous amount of pronouncedly personcentric biometric information others can glean from one's face, anonymity often manifests itself in facelessness.[37] Yet as quite compellingly implied etymologically, it is most explicitly evidenced in namelessness, as so famously exemplified by the French and British memorial tombs erected at the end of World War I in honor of the so-called Unknown Soldier[38] and thereby symbolically embodying the ultimately impersonal envisioned nature of those personcentrically *unspecified* individuals. As U.S. Senator Amy Klobuchar recounted to the joint session of Congress on January 6, 2021, right before the counting of the Electoral College ballots in order to officially certify Biden's presidential election victory—a historic session interrupted for several hours by the infamous storming of the U.S. Capitol,

> My friend Roy Blunt . . . years ago found . . . a bust of a man at the top of a bookcase [and discovered] that no one knew who this guy was. . . . At the time, our leaders thought this man important enough that they would warrant a statue for him, but today no one knows who he is. Senator Blunt's message to school kids and senators alike that visit his office when he shows them the statue, "*What* we do here is more important than *who* we are."[39]

In other words, she thereby allegorically implied, public servants' pronouncedly impersonal identities as the effectively substitutable incumbents of the essentially generic social positions they occupy as elected officials are ultimately far more critical than who they personally are as specifically identifiable individuals.

4

Impersonalization

The king is dead. Long live the king!

Having identified the fundamental formal properties of the kind of social interactions and relations we consider impersonal, we can proceed now to examine the main constitutive ingredients of the actual process of producing such impersonality, namely *impersonalization*.

Essentially a process of attention management, impersonalization ultimately boils down to *foregrounding individuals' social identity* (that is, "what" they are) while downplaying and thereby *backgrounding their personal identity* (that is, specifically "who" they are).[1] In other words, it involves attending to their generic features while disattending[2] their singularity.

In short, impersonalization implies disregarding individuals' specificity, thereby effectively *genericizing* them.

Typification

As we have seen, the distinction between the personal and impersonal visions of personhood presupposes a fundamental epistemic contrast between viewing people as unique individuals and as presumably "typical" (and, as such, "representative") members of particular social categories or groups. In marked contrast to the assumed *a*typicality of charismatic leaders, for instance, typicality is thus a fundamental formal property of impersonality.

The process of epistemically transforming specific individuals into presumably typical representatives of particular social categories has been aptly dubbed by Alfred Schutz *"typification"*[3] and is perhaps best

Don't Take It Personally. Eviatar Zerubavel, Oxford University Press. © Eviatar Zerubavel 2024.
DOI: 10.1093/oso/9780197691335.003.0004

exemplified by the mental act of *diagnosing*. Rather than regarding their patients as singular, unique individuals exhibiting specific symptoms (a dizzy spell, chest pain, weight loss), for example, doctors effectively consider those symptoms typical instances of certain generic clinical categories. As such, they come to respectively view those individuals as having an "ear infection," having suffered a "heart attack," or having developed "cancer." Furthermore, essentially applying the socio-epistemic tactic of *labeling*, they mentally catalog the various patients they treat as presumably typical "anorexics," "diabetics," or "drug addicts," for instance.

Consider also in this regard some of the professional tips provided by real estate agents to home sellers on how to in fact typify and thus impersonalize their house or apartment so as to help potential buyers envision (and thereby actually imagine) it as theirs. Effectively downplaying its pronouncedly personal idiosyncrasies, they can thus help give it an ultimately genericized, "unmarked,"[4] presumably "neutral"[5] look. After all, "the fewer clues you leave that *a specific person* lives in your home," so goes realtors' advice, "the easier it will be for a buyer to imagine living there."[6] Therefore,

get rid of friends' and relatives' Christmas photos, postcards, or baby announcements on the refrigerator or mantel.

Remove *distinct* artwork, décor, and collections. A collection . . . is a statement about *you* and what *you* value or spend your time doing. Such *personal* statements detract from selling your house.

Put away signs of religion, politics, or ideology. Your beliefs (or those of your children) may speak well of you, but *they are highly personal* and close another door to buyers thinking of the house as potentially theirs.[7]

Impersonalizing the specific (and, as such, idiosyncratic), in short, implies typifying and thus genericizing it. In other words, impersonalization is essentially a process of *de-singularizing* specific persons and social situations, thereby ultimately de-individuating them.

Such efforts to de-singularize and thus genericize the otherwise specific (and therefore potentially regarded as personal) also characterize,

34   DON'T TAKE IT PERSONALLY

for example, the relationship between sex workers and their clients, a pronouncedly impersonal social relationship effectively "reduced to its purely *generic* content" and thereby consisting only of "what *any member of the species* can perform and experience."[8] In other words, "it is a relationship in which the most contrasting personalities are equal and *individual differences are eliminated.*"[9] As such, in sharp contrast to romantic relations, for instance, it is indeed a relationship between two ultimately generic "impersons," so to speak.

Consider also in this regard the use of the *stare decisis* principle in common law. After all, envisioning previous court decisions as presumably typical judicial "*precedents*" presupposes an epistemic process of disattending their specificity (and therefore singularity) and foregrounding their generic (and, as such, non-idiosyncratic) features that can then be generalized and thus judicially reapplied to analogous ("parallel")[10] and thereby supposedly "similar" subsequent legal cases.

Standardization

Furthermore, as evidenced, for instance, with regard to self-defense, legal liability is often decided in relation to the presumed opinion of some hypothetical "reasonable person," such as when jurors are explicitly instructed by the judge to consider the question, "What would a reasonable person do in similar circumstances?"[11] Like Adolphe Quetelet's classic statistical vision of the ultimately generic "average man,"[12] or for that matter economists' equally hypothetical "rational man," such "reasonable person" is *standardly* envisioned as an epistemic "representative" of a pronouncedly generic category, thereby transcending any unique idiosyncrasies. Such a characterization, indeed, also applies to "*proxies*," as respectively exemplified in the worlds of fashion, film, as well as traditional medical research design by the way we use professional models (let alone faceless and thereby *personal-identityless* manikins), stuntmen, and white male so-called standardized patients as generic, presumably typical *stand-ins* for specific individuals.[13]

Given that standardness is one of the fundamental features of impersonality, it is hardly surprising that *standardization* is indeed a major constitutive ingredient of the process of impersonalization. By effectively making social interaction more scripted and formulaic (that is, "routinized"),[14] it thus helps promote the predominance of the generic and thereby presumably typical over the specific and therefore often idiosyncratic. And since charisma, ultimately emblematizing personalness, is fundamentally antithetical to any form of routine,[15] it is thereby quite telling that the very term used by Weber to characterize the process of the impersonalization of authority was, indeed, "the *routinization* of charisma."[16]

Standardization defies the very notion of a unique, distinctive personal identity. It thus champions *uniformization*,[17] such as when all applicants for a particular position receive *equal* consideration, when employees get standard across-the-board salary raises rather than personalized bonuses based on individuals' distinctive merit, and when product designers try to ensure that "a size 6 shoe is," indeed, "a size 6 shoe."[18] Just as illustrative in this regard are the pronouncedly standard, protocol-based professional *procedures* routinely followed by pharmacists, pollsters, and accountants, for instance, or for that matter the effectively standardized "Apgar score" used by pediatricians to assess individuals' general well-being at birth and the ultimately formulaic scripts used by both obituarists and tombstone designers when they die.

By the same token, in medicine, standardization manifests itself in the practice of following routine (and, as such, pronouncedly impersonal) procedures rather than clinicians' essentially idiosyncratic personal intuition (or, for that matter, "instinct").[19] Likewise, in law, it is evidenced in the practice of following standard judicial procedures effectively designed to minimize, if not entirely eliminate, strictly personal elements of adjudication such as "wisdom" or "insight." Based on nonspecific, general principles, the law's "spirit of formalistic impersonality"[20] is thus ultimately designed to free judicial justice from depending on independent-minded, maverick (that is, figuratively "unbranded") judges. Rather than having to rely on brilliant yet highly unpredictable charismatic individuals such as the biblical King Solomon, who purportedly proposed literally cutting a baby in two in order to be able to distinguish genuine claims to motherhood from false ones,[21] it favors standard adjudication procedures

36 DON'T TAKE IT PERSONALLY

taught in standard training institutions such as officially accredited law schools.

Indeed, that is one of the most significant features of what we consider "professionalism," as evidenced by the standardization of individuals' professional "credentials," wherein qualifications for eligibility for any given position are explicitly articulated in pronouncedly impersonal terms of standard types as well as amounts of formal training routinely documented in ultimately standardized, effectively formulaic résumés. After all, it is the formally trained meteorologist rather than the exceptionally intuitive prophet that a television station would be much more likely to hire to present its weather forecasts, for instance, and one's having paid for the professional services of an officially licensed MD rather than a charismatic folk healer or fortune teller that insurance companies would be more likely to reimburse. By the same token, it is the job candidate with a conventional PhD degree that universities would be much more likely to hire than the more brilliant one who has nevertheless had no formal education. That also underscores the significant role of *standardized tests of professional expertise*, formally backed by standard official certification diplomas, in the pronouncedly routinized process of licensing prospective lawyers, social workers, architects, and clinical psychologists.[22]

Institutionalization

One of the foremost features of any social order based on something other than charisma is the *impersonalization of authority* so that people, "insofar as they obey a person in authority, *do not owe this obedience to him [sic] as an individual, but to the impersonal order.*"[23] That implies the "transformation of charisma into an institution,"[24] a special process aptly dubbed by sociologists "*institutionalization*." "As permanent structures and traditions replace the belief in the revelation and heroism of charismatic personalities," in other words, "charisma becomes part of an established social structure."[25] Instead of a largely unpredictable (and therefore, as we shall see, also highly unstable) personcentric social order, that presupposes a pronouncedly impersonal one based on people's institutionalized positions rather than individual personhood. Loyalty, for instance, thus implies a "strong and faithful attachment to a person *not so much by reason of his* [sic] *personal character as of his official position*,"[26] as William Stubbs so succinctly put it. In other words, it does not involve "a relationship to a *person . . .* but rather is devoted to *impersonal . . .* purposes."[27] As such, it is part of a social order that revolves around various impersonal *institutions* such as "the court," "the Crown," and "the Holy See" rather than any specific judge, monarch, or pontiff.

In sharp contrast to charismatic authority, which is effectively based on a strictly personal vision of personhood, what Weber characterized as *legal authority*[28] is grounded, instead, in a pronouncedly impersonal, law-centric rather than personcentric one. The "purest" manifestation of this type of authority one sees in *bureaucracy*,[29] a particular form of social organization the very term (derived from *bureau*, the French word for "office") for which literally conveys the idea of "the rule of the office," which, as characterized by "the linkage of charisma with the holding of an *office*,"[30] an "*office charisma*,"[31] so to speak, most compellingly captures the essence of a strictly impersonal vision of personhood. Charisma, in short, is thus fully impersonalized and thereby institutionalized when it is indeed "transformed into a quality that is . . . *attached to the incumbent of an office . . . regardless of the persons involved*."[32]

Consider, for instance, in this regard spiritual leaders. "The bishop, the priest and the preacher," after all, are thus

> in fact no longer, as in early Christian times, carriers of a purely *personal* charisma, which offers other-worldly sacred values under the personal mandate of a master. . . . They have become *officials* in the service of . . . a purpose which in the present-day "church" appears . . . *impersonalized*.[33]

The authority attached to his "office," in other words, is thus effectively "emancipated from the personal qualities of the priest."[34]

Even the pope's presumed infallibility, indeed, is actually attached to his position as a pope[35] rather than to him as a specific person and, as such, is thereby effectively inseparable from his "office." In other words, it is based on the traditional belief that in doctrinal matters, he in fact

38   DON'T TAKE IT PERSONALLY

exercises his authority not as a specific individual (that is, personally) but *ex cathedra* ("from his seat") or *ex officio* ("as a result of his position") as the pope (that is, strictly impersonally).

The very same social logic applies to secular leaders as well. After all, legal authority is attached not to specific individuals but ex officio— that is, to their official positions *qua* chief executive officer, platoon commander, sheriff, or teacher.

As so compellingly exemplified by formal "job descriptions," "offices" clearly exist quite independently of their particular occupants at any given time. And indeed, rather than personcentrically target specific individuals, "job searches" for potential incumbents of such pronouncedly impersonal positions are thus designed to figuratively "fill" those "*slots in the social structure*" with candidates who would best "fit" them, just as they do standardized "extra-large" T-shirts or "size ten" shoes.

At the heart of any such institutionalized system of impersonal "offices" lies the notion of the ultimately standardized *career*,[36] any "movement" within which is strictly regulated by pronouncedly scripted, unmistakably impersonal conditions for promotion[37] formally articulated in terms of a standard sequence of "steps" one has to figuratively go through (such as becoming a hospital resident only after having completed one's internship) as well as a standard pace of mobility from one such "step" to the next.[38] Such a notion, in short, presupposes a fundamentally scripted *institutionalized structure of professional mobility* essentially designed to keep exceptional and therefore ultimately atypical individuals from being promoted in a nonstandardized, effectively personcentric manner, as when trying to come up "too soon" for partnership at one's law firm, move "too fast" between becoming a one-star and a two-star general, or "skip" the academic rank of assistant professor altogether. As such, institutionalization perfectly emblematizes the triumph of the standard and thus impersonal over the special and therefore personal.

Substitution

As so explicitly exemplified by formally institutionalized positions such as "*substitute* teacher," "*alternate* juror," "*deputy* chair," and "*vice* president," institutionalization presupposes the functional substitutability of the various specific occupants of any given generic "slot in the social structure." The very existence of such official positions, after all, underscores the fact that teachers, jurors, chairpersons, as well as presidents are ultimately *replaceable* (as, for that matter, is every airline pilot, dentist, radio announcer, and marriage counselor).

In sharp contrast to charisma, which is fundamentally antithetical to the very notion of substitutability, one of the distinctive characteristics of bureaucracy, as well as of institutionalization in general, is the effort to maximize functional *interchangeability* by effectively standardizing the social expectations from *all* occupants of a given position. Indeed, bureaucracy abhors supposedly indispensable "stars," who, as such, are ultimately considered irreplaceable. Whereas in sport and the performing arts, for example, substitutes' benches and understudies notwithstanding, one would never expect anybody to actually "replace" a Nadia Comăneci, Johan Cruyff, Charlie Parker, Rudolf Nureyev, Charlie Chaplin, or Billie Holiday, one of the major goals of bureaucratic organizations such as banks, churches, hospitals, armies, and schools is to minimize the presumed indispensability and therefore irreplaceability of any specific cashier, pastor, physician, battalion commander, or instructor as much as possible. As Ukraine's defense minister Oleksii Reznikov explained during his country's 2022 war with Russia, even "if they kill me, nothing will change, because . . . *someone else will take my position*, and we will continue in the struggle."[39]

Needless to say, the very notion of "routinizing" and thereby institutionalizing charisma presupposes its presumed transferability from any specific occupant of a given generic social position to the next.[40] A perfect example of such institutionalized transfer of authority is the way "succession" is traditionally organized in monarchies, where royal authority is assumed to derive not from the specific monarch's supposedly "inner" and thereby presumably personal qualities but, rather, from his or her genealogical position in some collectively envisioned official "*line of succession*."[41] Successors are thus assumed to effectively "inherit" their authority from their predecessors in a non-personcentric, pronouncedly impersonal manner. Such "*institutional heredity*," so to speak, implies an

40   DON'T TAKE IT PERSONALLY

essentially impersonal "hereditary ('lineage,' 'dynastic') charisma,"[42] ultimately independent of the specific individual occupying the position at any given time.[43]

Thus, as exemplified, for instance, by the British royal line-of-succession charts that popped up soon after Queen Elizabeth II died, when her eldest son was formally proclaimed "King Charles III" and the entire royal family figuratively moved one step up in the "line," there is an officially envisioned sequence of several dozen generic "pre-royal" slots in the social structure of the British monarchy occupied at any given point by several dozen specific individuals. Yet specifically *who* at that point occupies a particular slot in that "line" is only secondary in its significance to *which slot* he or she occupies.

Like royal and other genealogically based forms of "traditional"[44] authority, legal authority, too, is transferred through institutionalized "lines of succession" consisting of series of pronouncedly impersonal "slots in the social structure." Such officially envisioned "lines" exist entirely independently of the specific incumbents of those "slots" at any given time, as exemplified by the quasi-genealogical[45] series of the generic positions of "Vice President of the United States," "Speaker of the U.S. House of Representatives," "President pro tempore of the U.S. Senate," "U.S. Secretary of State," "U.S. Secretary of the Treasury," and "U.S. Secretary of Defense," which is utterly independent of the actual "chain"[46] of their specific current occupants, namely Kamala Harris, Kevin McCarthy, Patty Murray, Antony Blinken, Janet Yellen, and Lloyd Austin. In a way, they constitute a fundamentally generic (and, as such, pronouncedly impersonal) figurative "script" featuring *any* specific future would-be-occupants of those positions in case any specific future U.S. president dies in office.

Nowhere has such institutionalized procedure of transferring political authority been captured more compellingly than in the iconically photographed 1963 swearing-in ceremony of President Lyndon Johnson on Air Force One just ninety-eight minutes after his immediate predecessor, John Kennedy, was officially pronounced dead. In fact, such fundamentally impersonal orderly transfer of power is considered one of the most cherished prides of non-charismatic political orders in sharp contrast to pronouncedly autocratic ones, as exemplified by the disturbingly personcentric aftermath of the U.S.

2020 presidential election, when a sitting president refused for the first time ever to concede his electoral defeat at the polls.

Writing plays a major role in helping promote interpersonal substitutability. Effectively embodying the notion of impersonal professional responsibility, it is the patient's chart, for example, that facilitates the transferability of clinical duty and accountability by helping hospitals provide patients with presumably continuous care despite numerous all-too-frequent staff turnovers.[47] The fact that every day before they leave the hospital doctors and nurses fill out progress notes on each of their patients helps minimize the obvious disruptive effects of such turnovers on nights, days off, weekends, holidays, and vacations. By providing their replacements with instant clinical information about their patients, such reports allow them to assume their professional responsibility for those patients from the very moment they arrive at the hospital.

Patients' charts also constitute the foundations of hospitals' institutional (and thus unmistakably impersonal) clinical memory,[48] as they essentially narrate patients' hospital careers in a seemingly single narrative, thereby downplaying the distinctive personal identities of the specific clinicians who, having treated them, actually wrote those progress notes. As such, those notes are therefore collectively (and thereby impersonally) produced by members of ultimately generic categories ("doctor," "nurse"), the specific "representatives" of which are actually considered effectively interchangeable with one another.

In helping make any specific hospital staff member practically replaceable, patients' charts thus constitute the functional equivalents of the literally scripted "lines" in a play that allow understudies to actually "fill in" for sick actors at a short notice, as well as of the musical scores that help make every member of an orchestra ultimately substitutable. In sharp contrast to unscripted, spontaneous behavior, such scripts thus embody our vision of pronouncedly impersonal generic positions, essentially separable from the specific individuals who actually occupy them at any given time, thereby effectively helping ensure interpersonal substitutability.

One of the foremost features of bureaucracy as well as of institutionalization more generally, in short, is the significant role of written, let alone printed, *documents* (organizational bylaws, affidavits, medical

42 DON'T TAKE IT PERSONALLY

prescriptions, minutes of meetings) that exist quite independently of the specific individuals who in fact produced them.[49] As such, we often attribute to them an aura of permanence which none of those individuals themselves actually have, thereby enhancing the perceived durability of the institutional positions they occupy.

Such *symbolic immortality*, so to speak, underlies the very notions of social "position" and "role." By essentially downplaying the distinctly personal aspects (and thereby also transcending the actual "shelf life") of its specific incumbents, we thus come to view that "slot in the social structure" as fundamentally immortal.

As a deliberate effort to defy the inevitability of individuals' mortality, such symbolic *immortalization* is spectacularly exemplified by the aforementioned phenomenon of *hereditary authority*. Indeed, as Simmel so brilliantly observed, the otherwise seemingly oxymoronic traditional proclamation, "*The king is dead. Long live the king*," for example, perfectly captures the envisioned immortality of institutional positions. Despite the obvious fact that its most recent specific occupant has actually died, the position "king" itself thus nevertheless remains symbolically alive:

> The attempt is made to *guard against all the dangers of personality*, particularly those of possible intervals between the important persons, by the principle: "The king never dies." . . . This newer principle . . . involves an extraordinarily significant sociological conception, viz., the king is no longer king *as a person*, but . . . *his person is only the in itself irrelevant vehicle of the abstract kingship*.[50]

The notion that "the king never dies" therefore implies that any specific monarch is thus regarded as but a temporary occupant of an essentially generic "deathless office."[51] Such symbolically immortal "office" is thereby ultimately unaffected by the mortality of any of its merely temporary specific occupants.[52]

One of the most significant cognitive implications of such symbolic immortality is the way we come to view the institutional positions currently occupied by *President* Biden, Japanese *Emperor* Naruhito, and *Pope* Francis, for example, as *the very same* generic "slots in the social structure" ("president," "emperor," and "pope") previously occupied by

IMPERSONALIZATION   43

President Abraham Lincoln in the 1860s, *Emperor* Tokugawa Ieyasu in the early 1600s, and *Pope* Gregory the Great in the 590s. Although respectively separated from each other by one and a half, four, and even fourteen centuries, we actually envision the two specific paired individuals in each of those three instances (Lincoln and Biden, Tokugawa and Naruhito, and Gregory and Francis) as but variously personified historical manifestations of *one and the same* generic structural as well as functional entity.

Downplaying the distinctness of each specific occupant of a given social position thus helps symbolically immortalize it, and the authority institutionally attached to it can therefore be transferred from one such specific individual to the next as many times as necessary without actually interrupting its envisioned continuity as a fundamentally generic and thereby impersonal quasi-dynastic[53] "line" or "chain" of officeholders. Only thus, indeed, do we come to respectively envision Biden, Naruhito, and Francis as the forty-sixth president of the United States, the 126th occupant of the Chrysanthemum Throne, and the 265th successor of Saint Peter.

Anonymization

One of the most prominent features of impersonality is envisioned "*groupness.*"[54] A product of our epistemic ability to downplay the singularity and therefore individuality of each specific member of a social group and thereby view the entire group as a single entity, it underlies the fundamental sociological vision, originally articulated by Herbert Spencer, of social quasi-organisms that exist independently of their specific individual constituents.[55]

De-individuation presupposes "*anonymization,*"[56] an epistemic process of *downplaying individuals' personal identity*, thereby making it difficult to tell specifically "who" (rather than generically "what," let alone "how many") they are, which renders them, of course, impersonal. Such effectively anonymized "groupness" is what we actually envision, for example, when watching an international soccer match or intercollegiate relay race. And what ultimately helps us envision identifiable national or collegiate "teams" on such occasions is the fact that

44 DON'T TAKE IT PERSONALLY

with the single exception of the goalkeeper in soccer, all team members are visually recognizable as such by wearing same-colored jerseys (or functionally equivalent same-colored caps in water polo games, for that matter).

As an exceptionally effective emblem of impersonality, uniforms, indeed, help lessen our perceptual reliance on what are, after all, among the foremost manifestations of individuals' singularity, namely their idiosyncratic and thereby distinctive, visually individuating personal looks. As etymologically evident, they are in fact designed to produce a semblance of *uniformity*.[57] That, indeed, is the anonymizing (and, as such, de-individuating) function of both school and military uniforms, monks' and nuns' habits, as well as prison jumpsuits.

The social phenomenology of "groupness" is further evidenced in conscious, deliberate efforts to *visually eliminate any trace of embodied individuality*.[58] As so spectacularly demonstrated in Leni Riefenstahl's film *Triumph of the Will*, which infamously documented the Nazi Party's 1934 rally in Nuremberg, Germany, a foremost manifestation of such literally envisioned de-individuation is the meticulously choreographed synchronization of individuals' motoric actions so that they ultimately all *perform the exact same action at the exact same time*. As pointed out by Michel Foucault, this is most strikingly evident, for instance, when troops march *in unison* in military parades, as the entire group literally "raises the same foot at the same time,"[59] thereby also proceeding at *the exact same pace* as a single entity. Such fundamentally collective (and, as such, pronouncedly impersonal) rhythm[60] is thus the inevitable product of all the group members marching "in step" (which also explains why one of the most common metaphors we use to characterize nonconformity, or excessive individuality, is, indeed, being "out of step").

Such vivid sensory production of envisioned groupness is likewise accomplished not only visually but also sonically when people transcend their embodied individuality by *relinquishing their distinctive voice* and letting it literally "blend"[61] with others', as when they sing (in a choir, a soccer stadium, a birthday celebration, or a sing-along event) or speak in unison. Such pronouncedly synchronized "joint speech"[62] is manifested, for instance, in group recitations of oaths of

IMPERSONALIZATION   45

allegiance, in repetitive chanting of slogans in protest marches ("Black Lives Matter!") and political rallies ("U S A! U S A!" or "Lock her up!"), in "Bravo!" shouts during standing ovations, as well as in public prayer (such as at Mass, when chanting the mantra *Om* in a yoga class, or when families say grace together before meals). Those are all ultimately collective (and, as such, also impersonal) situations in which a group of individuals *utter the exact same words at the same time*.[63] And as when people sing their national anthem or school's alma mater *together*, the joint production of unisonous sound on such occasions thus constitutes a vivid enactment of groupness.[64]

Needless to say, anonymization also helps promote discretion. As such, it plays a major role in efforts to impersonalize illicit sexual encounters such as ones conducted in masked orgies and public restrooms,[65] for instance. It likewise promotes the use of screens or curtains in confessional booths. A screen, after all, "renders individual confessants as *anyones*, obscuring . . . their otherwise meaningful personal identities and accentuating their gener[ic] status as sinner[s]."[66] Furthermore, in a complementary manner,

> Catholic authorities also use the anonymity of the screen to depersonalize the priest's power and authority so that *any* individual priest can stand *in persona Christi*—as [a] gener[ic] proxy for God. . . . The barrier gives the priest the freedom and power to *transcend his personal identity and assume an impersonal . . . status* as a voice of God. With regard to his mortal personal identity, he, also, could be anyone.[67]

Consider also the role of writing in anonymization. After all, in marked contrast to our pronouncedly distinctive voice, which both literally and figuratively emblematizes our identifiability as unique, specific individuals, a written document does not always reveal, and may in fact even help deliberately conceal, the personal identity of the specific person who actually authored it, as evidenced by anonymously written ransom notes as well as anonymously published op-eds, pamphlets, and even entire books. Even the information printed on the consent form we sign on our first visit to a given medical facility, indeed, is officially dissociated from the effectively anonymous

46 DON'T TAKE IT PERSONALLY

specific lawyer who actually drafted that form, let alone the specific receptionist who hands it to us.[68]

As so vividly exemplified by the confessional screen, the mask, and the tainted car window for that matter, anonymity, in short, implies *non-identifiability*. After all, one's improper behavior can actually hurt one's reputation only when one is *personally* identifiable, and anonymization (as when writing subversive graffiti on public buildings at night, using a voice distorter, or traveling incognito) helps minimize such identifiability. So, indeed, does *pseudonymization*, or the use of fictitious names, which is specifically designed to conceal individuals' personal identity (and as such, is in fact one of the major social services provided, for example, by witness protection programs).

Pseudonyms are occasionally also assigned by both journalists and social researchers in an effort to conceal their informants' and subjects' personal identity—a fundamentally anonymizing practice commonly known as "*de-identifying*" them. As such, it is the functional equivalent of the professional practice of concealing prospective authors' personal identity when their manuscripts are being "blindly" reviewed by scholarly journals. And it also complements the ultimately de-individuating common research practice of random sampling.

The effort to *randomize* individuals likewise helps impersonalize even conventionally personcentric acts such as giving presents, as so perfectly exemplified by the effectively de-individuating Christmas-gifting "secret Santa" practice, which basically genericizes both the gift's recipients, who are randomly assigned, and its givers, who are essentially anonymized. Nor, for that matter, is blood, sperm, or organ donors' personal identity typically revealed publicly so that, at least in theory, they can be impersonally envisioned as simply "*someone*."[69]

Dispassion

Furthermore, "by anonymizing applicants, contestants, or examinees who compete for some valued reward," points out Thomas DeGloma,

> we express the principle that the evaluation of individuals' performances and achievements should not be influenced by . . . any

IMPERSONALIZATION   47

prior *personal* relationship with the evaluator. . . . We create and use such *depersonalizing* procedures . . . treating others (who are often made to be *generic* "subjects" or "candidates") *as impersonalized anyones.*[70]

That implies displaying *dispassion*, which is in fact what people mean when they say "It's nothing personal."

Given that a major characteristic of personalness is in fact the expression of affect (such as toward friends, for instance), one of the most distinctive features of impersonality, by contrast, is therefore the display of what Talcott Parsons famously identified as "*affective neutrality.*"[71] Nowhere is such display more demonstrably exemplified than in bureaucracy, which claims to "eliminat[e] from official business love, hatred, and all purely personal, irrational, and emotional elements."[72] Thus, for example, while "you might kiss or hug a close friend on greeting him on the street . . . you would not do the same to the next client in line in your job as a clerk at the department of motor vehicles."[73] As Weber, indeed, characterized bureaucracy's "spirit of formalistic impersonality," it ultimately manifests itself in acting

without hatred or passion, and hence without affection or enthusiasm. The dominant norms are concepts of straightforward duty *without regard to personal considerations.* Everyone is subject to formal *equality of treatment*; that is, everyone in the same empirical situation. This is the spirit in which the ideal official conducts his [sic] office.[74]

Such neutrality, as so compellingly evidenced in the conscious effort to appear impartial, constitutes a critical element in the kind of conduct we indeed deem "professional."[75]

Thus, for example, we expect such display of *impartiality* from instructors grading, preferably "blindly," their students' exams,[76] as well as from the doctors who treat us:

Affective neutrality is also involved in the physician's role as an applied scientist. The physician is expected to treat an objective problem in objective, scientifically justifiable terms. For example, *whether he*

48 DON'T TAKE IT PERSONALLY

likes or dislikes the particular patient as a person is supposed to be irrelevant, as indeed it is to most purely objective problems of how to handle a particular disease.[77]

By the same token, as evidenced, for instance, by the public outrage over the brutal police killings of Eric Garner and George Floyd, we likewise expect police officers to disentangle their personal feelings (such as hatred or rage) from the way they are supposed to handle individuals they try to arrest.

Given our trust in the "supposedly impartial and impersonal character of justice," thereby presuming that judicial institutions indeed "ac[t] on rule and *not upon impulse*,"[78] we likewise expect such display of impartiality from judges. After all, "according to legal tradition, the ideal judge is entirely dispassionate."[79] To quote Thomas Hobbes, he needs to be able to "divest oneself of all fear, anger, hatred, love and compassion,"[80] all of which we conventionally associate with personalness. Judges' implicit message to defendants they proceed to convict, therefore, is "I convict you not because I personally dislike you but because that is how I, or for that matter *any other judge in my place*, would have treated *any other case such as yours*."

One should not mistake the dispassion we expect instructors, doctors, police officers, and judges to professionally display, however, for what they actually feel. After all, it is not that the specific individuals occupying those social positions in fact lack any feelings. Indeed, they often *do* feel anger, sadness, disappointment, frustration, or even disgust,[81] yet those feelings are socially considered irrelevant and, as such, are supposed and therefore expected to be officially disattended.[82] Thus, when judges personally dislike particular defendants, for instance, they are professionally expected to essentially disregard that feeling. What they actually feel toward them is officially deemed "beside the point" and, as such, is not supposed to matter at all.

Effectively exemplifying the notion of "emotional labor,"[83] what judges (or, for that matter, instructors, doctors, and police officers) are professionally expected to do on such occasions is "manage" those feelings by socially regulating them.[84] For impersonalizing the judge–defendant relationship, in other words, the professional ideal is therefore the so-called emotionally well-regulated judge.[85]

Given the way we often view sex as fundamentally personcentric, displaying dispassion may also include precautionary efforts to *de-eroticize* impersonal social situations that might otherwise potentially be misconstrued as personal. By insisting that their clients use condoms, a conventional emblem of both literal and figurative social distancing, sex workers, for example, thus also help impersonalize their fundamentally professional encounters with them.[86] By the same token, gynecologists usually try to preventively ensure that their strictly clinical physical contact with their patients' intimate parts would not be misperceived as sexual and therefore personal. The avoidance of eye contact, the use of rubber gloves as well as a strictly technical vocabulary, let alone the presence of a nurse chaperone, for instance, are some of the professional measures specifically designed to help de-eroticize and thereby impersonalize doctor–patient interactions in such otherwise potentially mistakenly sexualizable professional situations.[87] So, for that matter, are "the examinee's undressing out of sight (usually behind a screen) and continued partial covering (usually with a sheet)" designed to help "segregate her vagina from its bodily context" and thereby "to sever the physical area of technical concern below from the social area above."[88]

Consider also, in this regard, the so-called "social kiss," the very term for which, being semiotically "marked" by the adjective "social" (just like the adjectives "marital" in *marital rape*, "white-collar" in *white-collar crime*, and "reverse" in *reverse racism*),[89] is in fact specifically designed to convey that it is not meant to be perceived as a conventionally ordinary (that is, "romantic") kiss. Whereas a kiss on the lips, after all, is usually considered a sign of ultimately personal affection (as indeed also evidenced by the fact that sex workers often avoid it in their effectively professional interactions with clients), let alone erotic desire, a kiss on the cheek, by contrast, is conventionally perceived as a merely ritualistic gesture signifying the essentially dispassionate (and therefore de-eroticized), fundamentally impersonal relation between the giver and the recipient.[90]

As an emblem of de-eroticization, the social kiss exemplifies the sociomental act of "framing"[91] conventionally personcentric, otherwise essentially sexual behavior, thereby semiotically transforming it into mere coquetry, its "lighter," effectively dispassionate (and, as such,

50 DON'T TAKE IT PERSONALLY

impersonal) form, which "has left far behind the reality of erotic desire" and is thus "embodied in the interaction" between individuals'

> mere silhouettes, as it were. . . . Where they themselves enter or are constantly present in the background, the whole process becomes a [personal] affair between two individuals. . . . But under the sociological sign of sociability from which the center of the personality's concrete and complete life is barred, coquetry is the flirtatious . . . play, in which *eroticism has freed the bare outline of its interactions from their . . . personal features.*[92]

In fact, notes Simmel, such

> *exclusion of the most personal element* extends even to certain external features of behavior. Thus, for instance, at an intimately *personal* . . . meeting with one or several men, a lady would not appear in as low-cut a dress as she wears without any embarrassment at a larger party. The reason is that at the party she does not feel involved *as an individual* to the same extent as she does at the more intimate gathering, and that she can therefore afford to abandon herself as if in the *impersonal* freedom of a mask.[93]

Wearing such a dress at a large cocktail party, in other words, thus conveys a fundamentally different message from what she would convey if she were to wear it on a romantic and thereby unmistakably personal date with a specific individual rather than at the essentially public and therefore ultimately impersonal encounter with effectively "anyone," as at the party.

5

Modernity and Impersonality

> The market community . . . is the most impersonal relationship . . . into which humans can enter with one another. . . . Its participants do not look toward the persons of each other. . . . There are . . . none of those spontaneous human relations that are sustained by personal unions.
>
> —Max Weber, *Economy and Society*, 636

An integral aspect of essentially any social relationship, impersonality is ultimately a transhistorical phenomenon, key elements of which one can actually identify in diverse historical contexts.[1] Indeed, it is hard to imagine any point in human history when social relations were conducted on a strictly personcentric basis. Even our prehistoric ancestors, after all, must have interacted with not only singularly envisioned individuals but also generically envisioned "elders," "women," "children," and "fellow clan members," for example.

Such genericity was further promoted by the invention of *language*, which underlies humans' ability to typify others in ultimately generic *categories*. In facilitating conceptualization, an epistemic process that presupposes the mental act of *generalizing*, language actually allows us to disregard individuals' idiosyncrasies and thereby transcend their singularity. The clash between Samuel and Saul depicted in the Bible more than two and a half millennia ago,[2] for instance, was thus not just a personal quarrel between two specific individuals but also a pronouncedly impersonal dispute between the occupants of two fundamentally adversarial—spiritual ("prophet") and political ("king")—leadership positions in ancient Israelite society. (As such, it was ultimately also analogous to "parallel"[3] disputes between the *prophet*

Don't Take It Personally. Eviatar Zerubavel, Oxford University Press. © Eviatar Zerubavel 2024.
DOI: 10.1093/oso/9780197691335.003.0005

52 DON'T TAKE IT PERSONALLY

Nathan and *King* David as well as between the *prophet* Elijah and *King* Ahab.)[4]

Yet the relative proportion of impersonality to personalness as two fundamentally complementary visions of personhood has also varied historically, and the impersonalization of humans' social life has in fact become particularly pronounced in the last several centuries, as social relations have come to "consist more and more of impersonal elements."[5] Indeed, while impersonality is definitely not a strictly contemporary phenomenon, it has nevertheless clearly become one of the most distinctive features of specifically *modern* social life.

Four major aspects of modernity—rationalism, urbanism, capitalism, and automation—have played a particularly critical role in the ever-increasing impersonalization of modern social life. Let us examine, then, how they have each helped impersonality become such a ubiquitous presence in our lives.

Rationalism

We have thus far identified standardness (with its particular emphasis on typicality) and bureaucracy (with its special emphasis on institutionalization, substitutability, and dispassion) as two particularly critical aspects of impersonality. As evidenced, for instance, by the pronounced prevalence of standardness in such widely disparate domains as technology, medicine, weather forecasting, jurisprudence, and education (let alone, for that matter, fashion, music, dance, and gymnastics), the impulse to standardize is a distinctive feature of modern life.[6] And so, after all, is bureaucracy.

Both standardization and bureaucratization, however, are actually but different aspects of the same pronouncedly modern process underlying the impersonalization of social life and dubbed by Weber *rationalization*.[7] Standardness has in fact been characterized as "one of the hallmarks of rationalization,"[8] and so, indeed, can bureaucracy.

Nowhere is the deep connection between *rationalism* and impersonality more starkly evident than in the avowedly objective (and, as such, highly impersonal)[9] spirit of modern scientific inquiry. Such emphasis

MODERNITY AND IMPERSONALITY   53

on *objectivity* is pronouncedly manifested, for instance, in the explicit effort to establish *interobserver reliability*, a distinctly modern methodological quest that, drawing on the bureaucratic notion of substitutability and thereby minimizing subjectivity, is specifically designed to promote "anyoneness" by eliminating any possible effects of inter-researcher variability, thus effectively implying that which specific individual actually collects, codes, or for that matter even analyzes the research data need not really matter. Given such methodological commitment to "interpersonal transferability," any given "observation does not depend on the observer's personal qualities or chance situation," as "anyone else in the same position who followed the same steps would observe the same facts."[10]

The pronouncedly modern spirit of impersonality underlying such objective and thereby supposedly "rational" approach to scientific inquiry is likewise evidenced by the distinctly modern prevalence of multiple-authored (and, as such, implicitly less subjective) scholarly publications, third-person self-referencing (such as replacing "we" with "the authors"), as well as the conventionally perceived superiority of statistically based survey research over both ethnographic and phenomenological (that is, "qualitative") and therefore more personal forms of social inquiry. Those are all products of the distinctly modern rationalist *repudiation of non-standardizable subjectivity* and the quest for a purportedly "objective" epistemic orientation, presumably devoid of any personal, ultimately *non-impersonalizable* feelings, biases, and intuition.

Urbanism

Impersonality is most characteristically (although by no means exclusively) an *urban* phenomenon. People who live in big cities usually develop "impersonal relationships with most of the people with whom [they] com[e] in contact."[11] That becomes particularly evident when one contrasts the kind of interpersonal relations that characterize social life in highly densely populated modern metropolitan centers such as Mumbai, Tokyo, São Paulo, and Shanghai with those more typical of life in villages or even small towns.[12]

54 DON'T TAKE IT PERSONALLY

A most distinctive feature of modern urban life is the fact that, given the large number of people they encounter on a daily basis as well as the growing prevalence of both structurally and functionally specialized social networks,[13] modern city dwellers tend to participate in more social relations although in a more fragmented manner.[14] Indeed, points out Louis Wirth, they usually come to know more people, yet in a necessarily more partial manner, as they typically interact with only "highly fractionalized aspects" of their selves.[15]

Such "segmental, functionally speci[alized] relationships,"[16] needless to say, necessarily promote impersonality.[17] The less of one's self a relationship encompasses, after all, the less it involves one's personhood in its "subjective totality"[18] and, as such, tends to be less personal.[19] Given that, it is hard to expect anything other than the pronouncedly dispassionate, emotionally flat *blasé* attitude that, as Simmel famously observed, modern city dwellers typically develop toward most of the people with whom they come in contact.[20] As Alvin Toffler sums this up,

> Rather than becoming deeply involved with the total personality of every individual we meet . . . we necessarily maintain superficial and partial contact. . . . What this means is that we form limited involvement relationships with most of the people around us.[21]

As one might expect, modern urban life also promotes anonymity, one of the fundamental constitutive elements of impersonality. After all, explains Lyn Lofland,

> as long as a human settlement remains small, it is a very simple matter for everyone living in it to know *personally* everyone else living in it. But as it begins to increase in size, this becomes more and more difficult until . . . knowing everyone in the settlement is totally impossible. And as the population continues to increase, the proportion of the total that any given individual can know *personally* becomes smaller and smaller until he [sic] is literally surrounded by strangers.[22]

A person living in a forty-eight-floor apartment building in Manhattan, for example, may thus not even know the names of many of his hundreds of neighbors who live in the very same building yet most of whom he occasionally gets to meet for only a couple dozen seconds on the elevator, if at all.

Given all this, the general level of personal trust one typically builds in a large city, where one is figuratively as well as literally but "a nameless face in the crowd," is considerably lower than what one usually comes to develop in a small town, where "everybody knows everybody."[23] By the same token, the very notion of a small-town (let alone village) blind date—or, for that matter, anonymous online dating (which in a big city, as Nora Ephron reminds us in her romantic comedy *You've Got Mail*, is in fact possible even within the same neighborhood)—sounds almost oxymoronic.

Nor, indeed, can one envision in a village or even a small town the kind of fundamentally impersonal sexual encounters between total strangers occasionally conducted in modern urban public restrooms,[24] so perfectly emblematized by the so-called glory holes specifically designed to accommodate oral and anal sex while literally excluding the rest of one's body, let alone self (and, as such, personal identity). Needless to say, anonymity plays a critical role in helping impersonalize such pronouncedly modern urban encounters.[25]

Thus, in sum, while modern urban life is by no means a necessity for the development of impersonality, it definitely helps foster and promote it.

Capitalism

Ultimately embodying the very essence of impersonality, the common expression "Don't take it personally" is often used almost interchangeably with the equally common equivalent cliché "Nothing personal; it's just business," thereby underscoring the strong association of the impersonal vision of personhood with *business*. Such implied contrast between the personal and the commercial[26] is most spectacularly evidenced in the *marketization* of social life.[27] Effectively reflecting the dispassionate and therefore fundamentally impersonal pursuit

56 DON'T TAKE IT PERSONALLY

of our "naked economic interests," the market, claims Weber, ideal-typically operates *"without regard for persons."*[28] Indeed, he points out, "the market community . . . is *the most impersonal relationship* . . . into which humans can enter with one another."[29] "The reason for *the impersonality of the market*," he adds, is

> its orientation to the commodity and only to that. Where the market is allowed to follow its own autonomous tendencies, its participants *do not look toward the persons of each other* but only toward the commodity; there are no obligations of brotherliness or reverence, and *none of those spontaneous human relations that are sustained by personal unions*. They all would just obstruct the free development of the bare market relationship.[30]

Nowhere is the market's pronouncedly modern "depersonalization of our bonds with others"[31] more starkly evident than in *capitalism*. As such, it parallels the predominantly modern "formalistic impersonality" of both bureaucracy and our fundamentally rationalist legal order.[32]

As famously observed by Karl Marx, in sharp contrast to autarky, which champions economic self-sufficiency, capitalism promotes *commodification*, which ultimately implies producing things not for their intrinsic "use value" but primarily as objects of commercial exchange (that is, for their "exchange value").[33] Rather than producing them, à-la Robinson Crusoe, strictly for one's own consumption, it thus involves expanding the imagined target of one's production, occasionally envisioning—such as in the case of Coca-Cola, blue jeans, or the "smart" phone, for instance—even humanity at large.

Indeed, most of what we consume today was actually *not produced specifically for us* (so that we are in fact "surrounded," to quote Simmel, "by nothing but impersonal objects").[34] The food we eat and the clothes we wear, for example, are for the most part *mass-produced* "for entirely *unknown* purchasers who *never personally* enter the producer's actual field of vision."[35] As befitting such *standardized production*, consumers are thus considered essentially interchangeable,[36] as so pronouncedly evidenced, for instance, in the fast-food industry,[37] prompting George Ritzer to in fact dub such distinctly modern form of ultimately impersonalized production "McDonaldization."[38]

The sharp contrast between standardized and *customized ("made-to-order") production*—which, being fundamentally personcentric, is explicitly designed to meet the distinctly personal and thereby pronouncedly idiosyncratic needs, as well as "taste," of a specific consumer—could not be more striking. As Simmel noted at the dawn of the twentieth century,

> Custom work, which predominated among medieval craftsmen and which rapidly declined only during the last century, gave the consumer a *personal* relationship to the commodity [which] was produced *specifically for him* [sic]. . . . Since the [decline of] custom production . . . the subjective aura of the product also disappears in relation to the consumer because *the commodity is now produced independently of him* [sic]. It becomes an objective given entity . . . autonomous of him [sic].[39]

The fundamental difference "between a modern . . . dress store and the work of a tailor who worked at the customer's house," he added, "sharply emphasizes the growing *objectivity* of the economic cosmos and its *impersonal* independence in relation to the individual consumer with whom it was originally closely identified."[40]

Needless to say, the commodified stands in marked contrast to the custom-made. Rather than a dress made *specifically for her*, the person who buys a dress in a department store needs to find there one actually mass-produced for *anyone* whose body fits a certain standard, generic, effectively impersonal size, as implied in the title of Claudio Benzecry's study of the modern shoe industry, *The Perfect Fit*.[41] "The buyer," in short, "has to adapt or else switch to another product."[42] Nowhere is the pronouncedly modern need to "*fit*" such standards more spectacularly exemplified than in the way modern consumers are in fact often characterized by the garment and shoe industries in ultimately generic and thereby impersonal terms such as "a size eight!"

Being useless in itself, *money* perfectly emblematizes the capitalist dominance of exchange over use value. Furthermore, as implicit in its anonymous and therefore fungible nature, it also promotes

58 DON'T TAKE IT PERSONALLY

interpersonal substitutability by effectively "transcending all individual distinctions,"[43] as so strikingly evident when contrasted with its considerably less fungible (and, as such, also much more personal) functional equivalent, the non-monetary gift. Whereas the latter "retains an element of the person who has given it"[44] as well as of its recipient,[45] money is usually "detached"[46] from both the payer and the payee.

Indeed, while non-monetary gifts are conventionally considered tokens of personal ties, money is the common medium of exchange in more impersonal relations.[47] Ideal-typically involving strictly commercial transactions between often anonymous (and, as such, ultimately interchangeable) members of generic social categories ("buyer," "seller," "customer," "cashier"), sex work, for instance, offers a perfect example.[48] Whereas with few exceptions[49] paying for sex would be conventionally considered deeply insulting between lovers, it is in fact the expected norm in what are, after all, unmistakably commercial transactions between sex workers and their clients, and it is hard to imagine, for example, a customer giving a prostitute a bouquet of flowers instead of paying her!

Automation

Furthermore, even a simple modern commercial transaction such as buying a dishwasher, for instance, already involves not just a single producer/seller but an entire production team, various middlemen (a wholesale supplier, a retailer), a delivery crew, as well as an installer. In other words, it also presupposes a lot of "*outsourcing*."

Yet the practice of outsourcing is by no means confined to commercial transactions alone. As Arlie Hochschild has so compellingly demonstrated,[50] it nowadays pervades even our traditionally most personal (and thereby least impersonal) relations.

Consider, for example, the commercial greeting card,[51] let alone its more recent digitized form, the so-called eCard. Using *readymade* (and therefore fundamentally generic), highly standardized (and, as such, pronouncedly formulaic) outsourced scripts even on ultimately personcentric occasions such as birthdays, bar mitzvahs, baby showers, and anniversaries, they thus emblematize the modern impersonalization of even traditionally personal relations, thereby effectively blurring the very distinction between the personal and impersonal visions of personhood.

The most common, let alone distinctly modern, form of outsourcing, however, is *automation*. Given the advent of industrialization in the eighteenth and nineteenth centuries, machines were indeed considered by Marx the ultimate capitalist means of production,[52] and, as such, have also been playing a major role in the impersonalization of modern social life, as so vividly exemplified by the introduction of the vending machine, the paradigmatic emblem of automated, *"person-to-imperson"* commercial transactions. The vending machine, observes Simmel,

> is the ultimate example of the mechanical character of the modern economy, since by means of the vending machine *the human relationship is completely eliminated* even in the retail trade where, for so long, the exchange of commodities was carried out between one person and another. The money equivalent is now exchanged against the commodity by a mechanical device.[53]

The rise of automation is likewise evidenced by the highly ubiquitous automated teller machine (ATM) as well as the recent proliferation of check-in and check-out machines in airports and supermarkets—all of which further exemplify the ever-increasing replacement of person-to-person by "person-to-imperson," machine-mediated transactions.

As further evidenced by the distinctly modern emergence of voicemail, asynchronous online teaching, and internet shopping, many traditionally person-to-person interactions are nowadays mediated by machines. And given the way bureaucracy promotes standardness, dispassion, and interpersonal substitutability, even our visions of adjudication and clinical diagnosis may soon transcend the confines of our traditional tacit assumption that judges and physicians actually need to be human, to the point where introducing their digitized, let alone AI, versions might be only a matter of time.

For a fictional glimpse into some possible future developments in the role of machines in impersonalizing our social life, consider also

60 DON'T TAKE IT PERSONALLY

Her, Spike Jonze's deeply disturbing cinematic portrayal of a romantic relationship between Theodore and "Samantha," a computer operating system personified, just like Amazon's virtual assistant "Alexa," by a disembodied female voice. When Theodore finally realizes that their seemingly personcentric relationship is in fact only one of 8,316 "personal" relations Samantha has been cultivating with her users, she insists that she is actually in love with "only" 641 others beside him! His deep sense of betrayal suggests that, even in a dystopian science-fictional world, maintaining 8,316 "personal" relations of which 642 also involve one's presumably personcentric affection nevertheless violates our tacit sense of the normative arithmetic of personalness and impersonality.

6

Impersonality and Its Discontents

> You find yourself in a society rampant with *dehumanization*, where people are barraged with crude *stereotypes* that are increasingly detached from the complexities of reality and make them feel *unseen as individuals*.
> —David Brooks, "Here's the Mind-Set That's Tearing Us Apart." Emphases added

Stability and Predictability

What are the benefits of impersonality? What do we gain, in other words, from impersonalizing so much of our social life?

A good place to begin examining the advantages of impersonality would be to try to imagine how humans must have envisioned their social surroundings prior to the invention of language. Through the use of conceptual *categories*, ultimately based on the epistemic process of typification, it is language, after all, that allows us to effectively disregard individuals' distinctiveness and thereby *transcend their singularity*. Without language, it would have been virtually impossible for us to envision others not only as specific individuals but also as our "great-grandparents,"[1] "superiors," "fellow academics," or "coreligionists." Nor, for that matter, would we have been able to distinguish between police officers' use of their ultimately role-based professional "authority" and of their sheer personal "force." By the same token, were it not for language, how would we be able to establish *non-personcentric*, generic rules as to what constitutes inappropriate behavior? In presupposing our use of language and thereby of categories, in other words, impersonality makes it possible for us to experience others not only specifically, as individuals, but also *generically*, as social beings.

Don't Take It Personally. Eviatar Zerubavel, Oxford University Press. © Eviatar Zerubavel 2024.
DOI: 10.1093/oso/9780197691335.003.0006

62 DON'T TAKE IT PERSONALLY

One of the major advantages of being envisioned impersonally and thereby not being singularized is the social luxury of remaining personally *inconspicuous*. After all, "if it seems good to be noticed," cautions a female employee at a predominantly male corporation, "wait until you make your first major mistake."[2] As anybody who has ever been stalked would attest, being personally "singled out" is not always what one would necessarily wish for oneself. Being noticed in a Nazi concentration camp, for instance, would actually put one "[in] danger of being selected as a victim of some punitive operation,"[3] and inmates indeed tried to avoid becoming singularized. Thus, for example, at roll call, one would often try to figuratively

> disappear somewhere in the middle rows. . . . In the marching column, one needed to get oneself a position roughly in the middle. The maxim was: avoid the exposed outer edges. . . . If one crossed the field of vision of the supervisors, one had to move . . . not too fast, not too slow.[4]

As likewise evidenced by suspects in police lineups as well as members of terrorist sleeper cells, both of whom indeed try to "keep a low profile" by "blending in" thereby effectively "hiding in the crowd,"[5] being the specific target of others' attention is desirable only as long as it is "positive" attention.

Next, consider the inherent drawbacks of charismatic authority, one of the major manifestations of personalness. Ironically, despite the fact that charisma is conventionally presumed to be based on the intrinsic, "inner" qualities of the particular individual to whom it is attributed, it actually lies in the eyes of its beholders and, as such, is effectively extrinsic to that person. In other words, charismatic authority is in fact a matter of sheer faith, and the specific individuals to whom it is attributed therefore actually "have" it only as long as their followers keep believing that they do!

Inevitably, given their complete dependence on those who attribute the charisma to them, "charismatic" figures are always under constant pressure to keep demonstrating to their followers that they indeed still possess those extraordinary "inner" qualities that they attribute to them. As we are reminded by Weber, "If proof and success elude the

IMPERSONALITY AND ITS DISCONTENTS   63

leader for long, if he appears deserted by his god or his magical or heroic powers . . . it is likely that his charismatic authority will disappear."[6] A "charismatic" leader must therefore "work miracles, if he wants to be a prophet" and "perform heroic deeds, if he wants to be a warlord."[7] The Greek kings of antiquity, for instance, thus "had to be not only brave, wise, and eloquent, but also distinguished in athletic exercises, and, so far as possible . . . superior carpenter[s], shipbuilder[s], and tiller[s] of the soil."[8]

As one might expect, that inevitably implies the fundamentally shaky nature of charismatic authority.[9] Whereas Herbert Hoover's presidential authority, for instance, was effectively protected by the U.S. Constitution throughout his term in office despite his lack of public popularity, charismatic leaders might need to miraculously bring water out of rocks (Moses) or conquer one country after another (Alexander the Great, Genghis Khan, Napoleon Bonaparte) in a constant, endless effort to convince their followers that they indeed still "have" the charisma that they attribute to them.

Needless to say, that implies the association of personalness with instability (and, conversely, of impersonality with *stability*)—an association particularly pronounced when one considers the tremendous challenge of managing succession,[10] as evidenced, for instance, by the desperate attempts made by some soccer fans to identify "a new [Diego] Maradona"[11] to whom they might be able to somehow "transfer" (and who would thereby presumably "inherit") the late Argentinian star's alleged charisma. After all, as so compellingly exemplified by the deeply chaotic political situation in Yugoslavia following Josip Broz Tito's death, for instance, or the rapid disintegration of the Inca Empire following the execution of Atahualpa by the Spaniards, the death of a charismatic leader, just like the act of removing the queen from a swarm of bees,[12] might in fact lead to a total systemic collapse. Indeed, what actually made it possible for Christianity and Islam to survive the deaths of Jesus and Muhammad was their remarkable success in having managed to effectively impersonalize their alleged charisma by respectively attaching it institutionally, and thereby non-personcentrically, to the papacy and the caliphate.

As further exemplified by George Patton, Bobby Fischer, and Elon Musk, for instance, let alone by jazz club and ballet company

64 DON'T TAKE IT PERSONALLY

managers' worries about their "featured" (and thereby effectively non-substitutable) saxophone player showing up late or prima ballerina getting sick, charisma often also engenders unpredictability. Impersonality, by contrast, involves supposedly "typical" role incumbents whom we expect to function in a pronouncedly standard (and, as such, fundamentally *predictable*) manner. Excessive personalness, as we have seen, also fosters cults of personality. Only establishing authority on a strictly non-personcentric, impersonal basis, indeed, can help mitigate the rise of Adolf Hitlers, Charles Mansons, and Donald Trumps.

Dehumanization

One can hardly miss the negative connotations implicit in references to a doctor's "cold, impersonal" bedside manner. Furthermore, given the deep connection between impersonality and both standardization and automation, nor, for that matter, is one likely to miss the negative undertones of portraying something as "cookie-cutter-like" or characterizing someone's behavior as "robotic."

Having considered the benefits of impersonality, let us also examine now its costs. What do we lose, in other words, by impersonalizing so much of our social life?

Consider, first, the moral implications of impersonalizing individuals' responsibility, thereby effectively allowing them to present themselves as but mere "cogs in the system." As so starkly evidenced by the Adolf Eichmann, My Lai, and Derek Chauvin trials, for instance, people sometimes shirk any responsibility for their wrongdoings by claiming that they actually acted not as specifically identifiable individuals but strictly impersonally, as incumbents of certain social roles such as a "soldier" or a "police officer." As a result, there are some situations in which in fact no one assumes responsibility for such conduct. It was such instances of *"floating responsibility,"*[13] indeed, that led Alain Resnais to end his classic Holocaust documentary film *Night and Fog* by featuring footage of Nazi atrocities followed by a montage of perpetrators and collaborators disturbingly denying any responsibility

IMPERSONALITY AND ITS DISCONTENTS   65

for them, and then posing the morally evocative rhetorical question, "Then who *is* responsible?"

Next, consider standardness, which, needless to say, suppresses our individuality, thereby fostering "a dull sameness."[14] The modern practice of basing medical treatment on standard diagnostic categories,[15] for instance, is indeed dismissed by critics as "cookbook" medicine that reduces medical care "from a clinical art to following a standard 'recipe,'" thereby effectively "making professionals' unique clinical skills and expertise redundant."[16] Instead of getting the individualized, personcentric treatment that their ultimately distinctive specific medical condition requires, patients are thus viewed by physicians (let alone insurance companies), those critics argue, "generically"— that is, "as one more instance of the same."[17] Using standard diagnostic categories and following standardized (and, as such, impersonal) treatment protocols, they claim, ignore each patient's specific medical condition, thereby preventing doctors from addressing its pronouncedly idiosyncratic and thus also more nuanced nature.

Such critique, in fact, actually applies to practically any act of categorizing (and thereby also mentally "*lumping*")[18] people, which ultimately implies envisioning individuals as by-and-large typical (and, as such, also effectively interchangeable) members of supposedly homogeneous categories. As is implicitly captured in the title of Sam Keen's book, *Faces of the Enemy: Reflections of the Hostile Imagination*,[19] that is particularly true of the way we often envision members of "out-groups."[20] While differentiating among (and thus epistemically individuating) members of social categories to which we believe we "belong" ("in-groups"),[21] we tend to homogenize in our imagination members of ones to which we do not,[22] thereby effectively typifying (and, as such, impersonalizing) them.

Our socio-cognitive tendency to mentally homogenize members of out-groups instead of viewing them as specific individuals is quite evident, for instance, in the way we sometimes mistakenly attribute information about particular individuals to other members of the social category to which they seem to epistemically "belong,"[23] thereby envisioning them as effectively interchangeable, as so disturbingly exemplified by erroneous eyewitness testimony.[24] By the same token, we occasionally also conflate their names,[25] such as when

66 DON'T TAKE IT PERSONALLY

mistakenly referring to someone named "Fernandez" or "Rosenbaum" as "Rodriguez" or "Finkelstein" (and thereby generically as a "Latino" or a "Jew"), or to a specific African American person by the name of a fellow African American co-worker at the same predominantly white workplace (and thereby generically as "black"). That also explains, for example, why the receptionist at my son's school once greeted me by saying "Hello, Mr. Romberg." Despite the fact that the actual Mr. Romberg, whose son also went to that school, was considerably older than me and did not resemble me physically, we nevertheless both had a heavy accent which, although mine was Hebrew and his was Spanish, evidently identified us in her mind as effectively interchangeable "foreigners."

Furthermore, envisioning people generically (that is, in terms of their fundamentally typified *labels* as "artists," "conservatives," or "baby boomers," for instance) also gives rise to category-based *stereotypes* that, being indiscriminately applied to individual members of those categories, are effectively "detached from the complexities of reality," thereby often "mak[ing] them feel *unseen as individuals*."[26] Attending primarily to a job applicant's ultimately impersonal gender-, age-, or ethnoracially based categorical membership, for example, thus reduces her to being viewed as a "woman," "twenty-something," or "black" instead of focusing on her personal credentials and qualifications as a specific individual.

Such one-dimensional, *reductive* view of people is indeed critiqued by "intersectionalists," who, ultimately objecting to the very notion of a single "master" status,[27] argue that presumably distinct social identities based on membership in a single category (race, gender, social class, sexual orientation) actually intersect, thereby generating more complex, fundamentally multidimensional categorical configurations based on people's *multiple* identities. Viewing individuals as supposedly typical (and, as such, essentially interchangeable) members of any single social category, they contend, inevitably results in ignoring other dimensions of their effectively distinctive personhood.

As exemplified, for instance, by racism, sexism, anti-Semitism, ageism, classism, and homophobia, such *stereotypification* often fosters *prejudice*, a fundamentally discriminatory epistemic bias targeting people *not as individuals* but as members of particular social

IMPERSONALITY AND ITS DISCONTENTS   67

categories. Whereas trust, for example, is usually organized in a predominantly personcentric manner, distrust often takes the form of *group*-based suspicion, whereby specific individuals are targeted based on their social rather than personal identity, such as on their nationality (as evidenced by the wholesale internment of Japanese Americans during World War II), race, religion, gender, or social class.

Such prejudice is manifested quite explicitly in ethnoracial *"profiling,"*[28] as exemplified by "stop-and-search" policies whereby specific individuals are frisked, arrested, and sometimes even fatally shot by law enforcement officials not because of any wrongdoings on their part but simply as a result of their membership in certain targeted social categories. As an Israeli aviation security expert puts it,

> Ethnic profiling is both effective and unavoidable. It's foolishness not to use profiles when you know that most terrorists come from certain ethnic groups and certain age groups. A bomber on a plane is likely to be Muslim and young, not an elderly holocaust survivor.[29]

The classic manifestation of group-based prejudice, however, are *"hate"* crimes, where people are killed simply for being members of particular social categories, as exemplified by femicide, pogroms, and ethnic "cleansings," let alone the infamous Ottoman, Hutu, and Nazi genocidal massacres of millions of Armenians, Tutsis, and Jews. Despite their conventional label, such crimes are actually motivated not by personal hatred toward particular individuals but by pronouncedly impersonal hostility toward entire social categories. Their victims, after all, are targeted not as specific individuals but as members of those categories (that is, *qua* "Gypsies," "transgenders," or "Asians"). In fact, the perpetrators of such crimes may not necessarily even know them before attacking them.

To understand how perpetrators of such "impersonal violence"[30] may not even care specifically who they target as long as he or she is a "prostitute," a "homeless person," or a "Jew," for instance, consider again our socio-cognitive tendency to envision people as typical (and, as such, ultimately interchangeable) "representatives" of the particular social categories to which they epistemically "belong" in our minds[31] rather than as specifically singularizable (and

68 DON'T TAKE IT PERSONALLY

therefore identifiable) individuals—a tendency likewise evidenced by the practice of collective punishment, where one is punished for acts committed by fellow members of the social category to which one "belongs." Indeed, argues Kathryn Olson, the manner in which stranger rapists and other "hate" criminals choose their victims actually parallels the way so-called sport hunters select their prey. The "hate" criminal thus views his victims

> as fundamentally *interchangeable*, not as distinct individuals.... [His] readiness to act violently rests on a perceived relationship to the generalized target group, not the unlucky, vulnerable individual member of it who opportunistically crosses the predator's path.[32]

Those victims, in other words, are therefore targeted *not as specific individuals but as epistemic "representatives" of particular social categories*—that is, in a strictly impersonal manner.

As so tellingly captured by the pronouncedly dismissive, tacitly racist expression *"They all look alike,"*[33] which parallels the way its users tend to view non-Disneyfied (and thereby non-personified, effectively clonelike) mice and ducks, for instance, typifying can also be highly demeaning. Indeed, by ultimately *objectifying* people as "typical" representatives of the particular social categories to which they epistemically "belong" while essentially disregarding their individuality, impersonalization is often considered dehumanizing.[34]

Such *dehumanization* also characterizes Weber's classic portrayals of both bureaucracy[35] and capitalism. "Such absolute *depersonalization*," he notes about the capitalist marketization of modern social relations, "is contrary to all the elementary forms of human relationship."[36]

Furthermore, as exemplified by our deep exasperation at receiving telemarketing "robocalls," let alone desperately trying to reason with an automated "customer representative," automation, too, fosters dehumanization. Indeed, that is also evidenced by our characterization of the way some servers recite the list of a restaurant's specials of the day in a standard, often literally scripted manner that hardly varies from one server (or, for that matter, customer) to another as "machinelike" or "robotic."

IMPERSONALITY AND ITS DISCONTENTS 69

Personalization

Not surprisingly, indeed, as exemplified by *personcentrically oriented* customer services that explicitly defy automation by offering callers the option of speaking to "a real person" rather than a machine, we sometimes try to add some *"personal touch"*[37] to otherwise impersonal situations. Instead of standardness and typicality, such attempts at "personalizing" involve efforts to emphasize *idiosyncrasy* and thereby *singularity*. In sharp contrast to impersonalization, *personalization* thus essentially boils down to backgrounding individuals' social identity (that is, "what" they are) while foregrounding their ultimately *distinctive* personal identity (that is, specifically "who" they are). In other words, it basically involves disregarding their genericity while highlighting their *specificity*.

Having considered the efforts to *im*personalize our social life, let us examine now the diametrically opposite effort to "personalize" it by trying to *project a semblance of personalness*.

Essentially defying capitalism, such efforts often take the form of *customization*.[38] Instead of being expected by producers to "fit" certain impersonal standards, consumers are actually offered "personalized" products[39] figuratively *"tailored"* specifically for them.

A critical component of customization is the element of *individual choice*, a major token of personalness. Even mass-producers, indeed, offer customers the opportunity to choose between a minivan and a sedan, a tight-fit and a loose-fit pair of pants, or a chocolate and a vanilla ice cream.[40]

Personalizing is likewise exemplified by Microsoft's and Zoom's efforts to help users customize their computer screensavers and video-call backgrounds, as well as by personal gift-giving. Indeed,

> even in societies where relations between individuals are becoming less and less personal, gift-giving often retains its "personal" character. . . . This personal character is associated not only with the donors but also with those who receive the gifts.[41]

Even in business relations, suggests one business coach, when looking for an appropriate gift one should therefore

70   DON'T TAKE IT PERSONALLY

avoid malls or shopping centres that cater to *generic* . . . cookie-cutter gifts and seek . . . more personal stores that offer *more personal* . . . gifts. . . . Don't just give *random, generic* gifts *anyone* would appreciate. Instead, give *personal* gifts that speak to the recipient's *unique* qualities.[42]

Such pronounced commitment to personalness has also given rise to "personalized learning," an explicitly nonstandardized pedagogical approach promoting adherence to a personalized curriculum based on the distinctive needs of each specific student. It is likewise evidenced in individualized, "person-centered" health care,[43] where, in sharp contrast to "cookbook" medicine, treatments are tailored to each patient's specific needs, as well as in individualized, "personalized diets" that explicitly defy standardized nutritional regimes.[44]

The spirit of personalization also accounts for efforts made by television networks to add to their reports of the ultimately impersonal statistics of earthquake, pandemic, and war casualties some distinctly personal stories about specific individuals. And it has likewise given rise to the jazz solo, in which the soloist delivers an improvised (and, as such, unmistakably distinctive) personal "statement" followed by a pronouncedly personcentric applause expressing the audience's appreciation of such unadulterated demonstration of singularity.

Given the close association of impersonality with anonymity, efforts to personalize also include highlighting individuals' *names*, as when requiring employees to wear a name badge as well as to personally introduce themselves when a customer calls on the phone. Such wish to personalize also underlies efforts to purposely publicize sexual assault survivors' personal identity instead of their social, ultimately impersonal identity as anonymous "rape victims,"[45] as well as the essentially parallel "Say Their Names" campaign to explicitly personalize victims of police brutality. It is likewise critical in situations in which one's individuality is overshadowed by the fact that one is habitually envisioned as part of an aggregate, as quite evident, for example, in the case of the Vietnam Veterans Memorial, which lists the names of each of the more than 58,000 Americans who were killed in the Vietnam War, thereby visually expressing the desire to singularize (and thereby personalize) them.

IMPERSONALITY AND ITS DISCONTENTS   71

Consider also in this regard the April 30, 2004 special edition of ABC's television news program *Nightline*, whose host, Ted Koppel, spent twenty-nine minutes simply reading the names of the 737 American casualties of the first thirteen months of the Iraq War in an effort to singularize each of them, thereby effectively personalizing the war's conventionally aggregated and thus ultimately impersonalized human cost.[46] Such heart-wrenching display of personalness likewise characterized Matthew McConaughey's White House press briefing following the elementary school shooting in Uvalde, Texas, in which he explicitly singularized the often-aggregated and thereby impersonalized tragedies of its nineteen youngest victims:

We met . . . Ryan and Jessica Ramirez. *Their 10-year-old daughter, Alithia . . . was one of the 19 children* that were killed. . . . Her dream was to go to art school in Paris and one day share her art with the world. . . . Her father . . . told her every single night . . . "Daddy is going to take you to SeaWorld one day." But . . . Alithia . . . did not get to go to SeaWorld.

We also met . . . the mom and the stepdad of *nine-year-old Maite Rodriguez*. And Maite wanted to be a marine biologist. She was already in contact with Corpus Christi University of A&M for her future college enrollment. Nine years old. . . . Maite wore green high-top Converse with a heart she had hand-drawn on the right toe. . . . These are the same green Converse on her feet that turned out to be the only clear evidence that could identify her after the shooting. . . . Maite wrote a letter [that] reads: "Marine biologist. I want to pass school to get to my dream college. My dream college is in Corpus Christi, by the ocean . . . I want to be a marine biologist."

Then there was *Ellie Garcia, a 10-year-old*. . . . Ellie loved to dance, and she loved church. . . . Smiling through tears, her family told us how Ellie loved to embrace. Said she was the biggest hugger in the family.

So where do we start? . . . We start by giving Maite a chance to become a marine biologist. . . . We start by giving Makenna, Layla, Maranda, Nevaeh, Jose, Xavier, Tess, Rojelio, Eliahna, Annabell, Jackie, Uziyah, Jayce, Jailah, Eva, Amerie, and Lexi—we start by

72 DON'T TAKE IT PERSONALLY

giving all of them our promise that their dreams are not going to be forgotten.[47]

Like referring to a person's name, adding a handwritten "personal" note at the end of a printed letter is semiotically designed to convey to its recipient that the letter was actually written by a *specific* person *specifically* to him or her. By the same token, consider also the way marketers often address potential viewers of their ads and commercials by using the second-person singular pronoun *"you,"* as well as the common use of the ostensibly personcentric salutations "How can *I* help *you*?" and "Have a nice day" at the beginnings and ends of service encounters. Indeed, notes Robin Leidner, service personnel

> are expected to *personalize* highly routinized interactions with eye contact and a smile, which supposedly constitute *"treating the customer as an individual."* ... The idea is to hide the routinization from service-recipients, to make them believe that the conversation is not scripted.[48]

Yet the conversation, of course, *is* in fact scripted. As exemplified by those unmistakably formulaic salutations, such "personal touch" is indeed standardized and, as such, only *pseudo*-personal.[49] "The "have a nice day" buttons, the waiter's "hope you enjoy your meal," and the receptionist's smile, Hochschild reminds us, are not really personal.[50]

In the dystopian world of *Her*, almost as unsettling as Theodore's perverted relationship with his computer operating system is the nature of his day job as a corporate ghostwriter of commercially outsourced "personal" letters, presumably modeled after that of a greeting card copywriter. Ultimately involving somebody anonymously scripting someone else's ostensibly personal feelings toward a family member or a friend, the greeting card indeed perfectly captures the spirit of personalization. Furthermore, as evidenced by their occasional use of cursive letters and deckle-edge paper,[51] greeting card producers sometimes also try to add an even more pseudo-personal touch to the card's pronouncedly standardized, formulaic text and design. Such *pseudo-personalization* adds yet another layer to the illusory character of such indisputably contrived personalness.

Like horoscopes and fortune cookies, greeting cards are designed to help project the illusion that a product that has in fact been manufactured in a standardized, essentially formulaic manner has nevertheless somehow been singularly produced with a specific recipient in mind. In that, they also resemble monogrammed jewelry, which, despite being actually mass-marketed, is nevertheless ostensibly designed to feature a specific individual's supposedly distinctive "personal" initials.

By the same token, when Netflix generates supposedly personalized ("Top Picks *for Eviatar*") lists of films that I am particularly likely to enjoy watching, its recommendations are actually only pseudo-personalized. Yet just like fraudulent "phishing" attackers, it nevertheless evidently believes that pseudo-personalization is indeed a most effective way of convincing me to actually follow them.

* * *

Championing personalness, some people actually question whether "not taking it personally" is even possible. "Why is it that when someone offends you," asks Linda Wheeler,

> the first thing they do to correct the situation is to say, "it is nothing personal"? . . . What is not personal when . . . they tell you about their selection of someone else for a job you really wanted, or when they say that they met someone new and do not care about you anymore? Why do they always add, "but do not take it personally"? How else can you take it?[52]

Yet as demonstrated throughout this book, impersonality is an integral part of our social life. After all, just like personalness, it actually constitutes one of our two equally fundamental complementary visions of personhood. The answer to the question whether "not taking it personally" is even possible, therefore, is a definitive "Yes." Indeed, it is no less possible than "taking it personally."

Notes

Preface

1. See, for example, Zerubavel 1979, 43-46; Zerubavel 1980, 164-66.
2. Zerubavel 2021.

Chapter 1

1. Sommers 2021. Emphasis added.
2. Ibid.
3. McGregor-Wood 2010. Retrieved March 8, 2021.
4. See, for example, Leschziner 2015, 123-46.
5. See also Durkheim 1966 [1897], 152–216; Simpson 2006.
6. Watt 2001 [1957], 18. See also 15–20.
7. Flaubert 1994 [1856], 47–48.
8. Hana Wirth-Nesher, personal communication.
9. Weber 1978 [1925], 241–45, 1111–56.
10. Zerubavel 2021, 66.
11. Weber 1978 [1925], 241.
12. Ibid., 243–44.
13. Ibid., 241–45.
14. Ibid., 246.
15. https://www.politico.com/story/2016/07/full-transcript-donald-trump-nomination-acceptance-speech-at-rnc-225974. Emphasis added. Retrieved February 1, 2021.
16. See, for example, Rubin 2017. Retrieved August 18, 2021.
17. See also Haberman 2021. Retrieved February 1, 2021.
18. Weber 1978 [1925], 242.
19. See, for example, Plott 2021.
20. See, for example, Strong and Killingsworth 2011.
21. Green 2021; Levin 2021. Both retrieved August 9, 2021.

76 NOTES

22. Wallis 2011, 50. Emphasis added. See also 48.
23. Ludovino 2017, 234. Emphases added.
24. Gabrielle LaFleur, personal communication.
25. See also Kolnai 1999 [1949], 96; DeGloma 2023.
26. Zerubavel 1997, 52.
27. Rich 1980.
28. Durkheim 1973 [1914], 152.
29. See also Lévi-Strauss 1966 [1962], 172–90.
30. Weber 1949 [1904], 89–111.
31. See, for example, Zelizer 2011 [2005], 313–14.
32. Saussure 1959 [1915], 13–15.
33. Iddo Tavory, personal communication.
34. Coser 1971, 180.
35. On the epistemic "invisibility" of the taken for granted, see Zerubavel 2015; Zerubavel 2018.

Chapter 2

1. See, for example, Paris and Katz 2022.
2. Simmel 1950 [1908a], 111. Emphasis added.
3. Ibid.
4. Ibid. Emphasis added. See also 108.
5. See also Cohen 1982, 36.
6. Mullaney 1999; Zerubavel 2018, 12–14, 43.
7. On that, see also Sorokin 1943.
8. Styron 1979.
9. See, for example, Durkheim 1966 [1897], 297–325.
10. Baron 2004, 393.
11. On the bureaucratic nature of the Holocaust, see Bauman 2000.
12. https://www.ifly.com/overweight-passengers. Retrieved June 9, 2021.
13. https://www.thefreedictionary.com/equality.
14. See also Simmel 1950 [1908b], 241.
15. Simmel 1950 [1908a], 111.
16. Y. Zerubavel 2014, 6.
17. https://www.britannica.com/topic/majoritarianism. Retrieved June 14, 2021.
18. Tocqueville 1945 [1835], 269, 276.
19. Mill 1956 [1859], 7. Emphases added.

NOTES 77

20. Aristotle, fourth century BC [1984], 183 (*Politics*, Book 6, Chapter 2, 1317b). Emphasis added.
21. Tocqueville 1945 [1835], 267–68, 272, 278.
22. Ibid., 265. Emphases added.
23. Simmel 1950 [1908b], 247.
24. Simmel 1990 [1907], 444.
25. Ibid. See also Simmel 1950 [1908b], 241.
26. Simmel 1990 [1907], 444.
27. Simmel 1950 [1908a], 111.
28. Y. Zerubavel 1995, 45; Y. Zerubavel 2014.
29. Y. Zerubavel 2014, 13.
30. Kanter 2008 [1977], 207–08.
31. Ibid., 210–11. See also Zerubavel 2018, 52.
32. Kanter 2008 [1977], 207. Emphases added.

Chapter 3

1. On the distinction between "doing" and "being," see Goffman 1961b; Mullaney 1999; Brekhus 2003.
2. Zerubavel 2018, 12. On verb-like and noun-like identities, see also Brekhus 2003.
3. Goffman 1963b.
4. Simmel 1950 [1908b], 248.
5. See also DeGloma 2023.
6. But see Goffman 1963b, 41–104; Turkle 1995.
7. See Goffman 1961b.
8. Pollard 2009.
9. See also Herschel McPherson's "While Black Project," https://vimeo.com/489500564. Retrieved March 8, 2021.
10. Goffman 1963b.
11. Suro 1987, A4. Emphasis added.
12. LaFleur 2021.
13. Kilpatrick 1974. Emphasis added. Retrieved September 15, 2021.
14. Festinger et al. 1952, 389. See also 382.
15. Berger and Luckmann 1967 [1966], 75. Emphasis added.
16. See also Mayntz 1970, 430.
17. Tajfel and Turner 1986.
18. See also Zerubavel 2018, 50–52.

78 NOTES

19. Ibid., 52.
20. Kanter 2008 [1977], 208. Emphasis added.
21. Ibid., 214. Emphases added.
22. On typicality, see Schutz and Luckmann 1973, 229–41. See also Berger and Luckmann 1967 [1966].
23. Quattrone and Jones 1980, 141.
24. See Rosch 1978.
25. Mayntz 1970, 428.
26. Gabrielle LaFleur, personal communication.
27. See also Ritzer 1996, 12; Wallis 2011, 48.
28. On that, see also DeGloma 2014, 12–13.
29. See, for example, Leidner 1993, 9, 13.
30. Zerubavel 1980, 165. Emphases added.
31. See also Cohen 1969, 108–09; Leidner 1993, 11.
32. Simmel 1990 [1907], 301.
33. On the relation between impersonality and collectivity, see also Durkheim 1973 [1914], 151, 162.
34. Zerubavel 1979, 44; Zerubavel 1980, 164.
35. See also Simmel 1950 [1917], 52–53.
36. Simmel 1898, 672.
37. See also DeGloma 2023.
38. See, for example, Mosse 1990, 94–97.
39. https://www.klobuchar.senate.gov/public/index.cfm/news-releases? ID=12CFAA0A-7062-4AC3-8A93-561416451B98. Emphases added. Retrieved January 26, 2021. See also https://www.klobuchar.senate.gov/public/index.cfm/2021/1/klobuchar-leads-debate-on-senate-floor-to-respond-to-baseless-objections-to-certified-electoral-votes.

Chapter 4

1. On "foregrounding" and "backgrounding," see Zerubavel 2015.
2. On "disattention," see Goffman 1961a, 19, 25; Goffman 1963a, 86; Emerson 1970, 76; Goffman 1974, 202, 207, 210, 214–15; Zerubavel 2015, 60, 63, 68.
3. Schutz and Luckmann 1973. See also Berger and Luckmann 1967 [1966].
4. On "unmarkedness," see Zerubavel 2018.
5. Ibid.
6. Bray 2019. Emphasis added.
7. Ibid. Emphases added.

NOTES 79

8. Simmel 1990 [1907], 376. Emphases added.
9. Ibid. Emphasis added.
10. See also Zerubavel 2021, 37–58.
11. See, for example, Alicke and Weigel 2021, 123.
12. Quetelet 2013 [1842].
13. See also Mulvin 2021, 145–81.
14. Leidner 1993. See also Ritzer 1996, 82.
15. Weber 1978 [1925], 246.
16. Ibid., 246–54.
17. Timmermans and Epstein 2010, 71.
18. Benzecry 2022, 217.
19. See also Timmermans and Berg 2003.
20. Weber 1978 [1925], 225.
21. See, for example, I Kings 3:16–28.
22. See Weber 1978 [1925], 218, 220, 999–1000.
23. Ibid., 218. Emphasis added.
24. Ibid., 1139.
25. Ibid.
26. Stubbs 1878, 508. Emphasis added.
27. Weber 1978 [1925], 959.
28. Ibid., 217–26.
29. Ibid., 219–20.
30. Ibid., 1139.
31. Ibid., 1139–41. See also 248.
32. Ibid., 1135. Emphasis added.
33. Ibid., 959. Emphases added.
34. Ibid., 249.
35. Ibid., 221.
36. Ibid., 220, 963.
37. Ibid.
38. See, for example, Zerubavel 1979, 5–9.
39. Melman 2022. Emphasis added. Retrieved October 30, 2022.
40. See also Weber 1978 [1925], 248.
41. See also Zerubavel 2011, 20, 118–21.
42. Weber 1978 [1925], 248, 1137–38.
43. See also Simmel 1898, 674.
44. Weber 1978 [1925], 226–31.
45. Zerubavel 2011, 118–30.
46. Ibid., 21–23, 125.
47. Zerubavel 1979, 45–46.

80 NOTES

48. See, for example, Zerubavel 1997, 93.
49. See also Weber 1978 [1925], 219, 957; Zerubavel 1980, 165; Zerubavel 1997, 93.
50. Simmel 1898, 673. Emphases added. See also Simmel 2009 [1908], 462–65; Kantorowicz 2016 [1957].
51. Simmel 1898, 673.
52. See also Zerubavel 1979, 43.
53. Zerubavel 2011, 118–27. See also Kantorowicz 2016 [1957], 317–36.
54. See, for example, Tajfel 1981, 237.
55. Spencer 1969 [1876], 8, 15–17. See also Simmel 1898.
56. Schutz 1967 [1932], 186. See also Schutz and Luckmann 1973, 79–84; Berger and Luckmann 1967 [1966], 32–33; DeGloma 2023.
57. Fussell 2002, 3. See also 20, 141.
58. See, for example, Dubin 1990.
59. Foucault 1979 [1975], 151.
60. Ibid., 151–52.
61. See also Hall 1906, 13, for instance.
62. Cummins 2018a; Cummins 2018b, 417–18.
63. Ibid.
64. Cummins 2018b, 418.
65. On the latter, see, for example, Humphreys 1970, 60.
66. DeGloma 2023, 47.
67. Ibid. Emphases added.
68. See also Zerubavel 1980, 164–65; Simmel, 1950 [1908d], 352–55.
69. But see the hilarious episode "The Anonymous Donor" in the HBO television sitcom *Curb Your Enthusiasm*. https://www.youtube.com/watch?v=_ _4vAVaL7h4. Retrieved November 6, 2021.
70. DeGloma 2023, 50. Emphases added.
71. Parsons 1951, 435.
72. Weber 1978 [1925], 975.
73. Appelrouth and Edles 2011, 29.
74. Weber 1978 [1925], 225. Emphases added.
75. Šmídová and Tollarová 2014, 847.
76. See also Downie 1971, 129.
77. Parsons 1951, 435. Emphasis added.
78. Mead 1918, 584. Emphasis added.
79. Maroney and Gross 2014, 142.
80. Hobbes 2016 [1651], 195. Emphasis added.
81. See also Maroney 2011, 1517–18.
82. On the social organization of irrelevance, see Zerubavel 2015.

NOTES 81

83. Hochschild 1983, 7. See also Steinberg and Figart 1999.
84. Maroney 2011; Maroney and Gross 2014, 142–43.
85. Maroney and Gross 2014, 142, 148.
86. See, for example, Horst 2022.
87. Emerson 1970; Horst 2022.
88. Davis 1983, 224.
89. Zerubavel 2018, 96, 28–29.
90. See also ibid., 12.
91. Bateson 1972 [1955]; Goffman 1974.
92. Simmel 1950 [1917], 51. Emphasis added.
93. Ibid., 46. Emphases added.

Chapter 5

1. On transhistorical theorizing, see Zerubavel 2021, 17.
2. See, for example, 1 Samuel 15.
3. On such "parallels," see Zerubavel 2021, 37–72.
4. 2 Samuel 12; 1 Kings 21.
5. Simmel 1950 [1908c], 318.
6. See also Zerubavel 1982; Timmermans and Epstein 2010, 71; Busch 2011.
7. Weber 1958 [1904–05], 13–26. See also Brubaker 1984, 2, 9.
8. Timmermans and Berg 2003, 8.
9. See also Brubaker 1984, 9.
10. De Swaan 2001. Emphasis added.
11. Cox 2013 [1965], 50.
12. See also Hochschild 2012, 1–17.
13. Mayntz 1970, 428. See also Schutz and Luckmann 1973, 299–318; Zerubavel 1997, 17–19.
14. Mayntz 1970, 428.
15. Wirth 1938, 12.
16. Mayntz 1970, 429.
17. Wirth 1938, 12; Mayntz 1970, 429.
18. Simmel 1950 [1908c], 318.
19. Toffler 1974 [1970], 96–99.
20. Simmel 1950 [1903], 414.
21. Toffler 1974 [1970], 96–97.
22. Lofland 1973, 9-10. Emphases added.
23. See also Simmel 1950 [1903], 415.

82 NOTES

24. See, for example, Humphreys 1970.
25. Ibid., 60.
26. See also Horst 2022.
27. See, for example, Hochschild 2012.
28. Weber 1978 [1925], 975. Emphasis added.
29. Ibid., 636. Emphasis added.
30. Ibid. Emphases added.
31. Hochschild 2012, 224.
32. Brubaker 1984, 21. See also 3.
33. Marx 1967 [1867], 35–83.
34. Simmel 1990 [1907], 460.
35. Simmel 1950 [1903], 411. Emphases added.
36. See also Lampel and Mintzberg 1996, 25.
37. See, for example, Leidner 1993, 11.
38. Ritzer 1996.
39. Simmel 1990 [1907], 457. Emphases added.
40. Ibid. Emphases added.
41. Benzecry 2022.
42. Lampel and Mintzberg 1996, 25.
43. Simmel 1990 [1907], 376.
44. Ibid.
45. Mauss 1967 [1925]; Schwartz 1967.
46. Simmel 1990 [1907], 376.
47. See also Brubaker 1984, 19. On the conventional nature of that difference, however, see Zelizer 1996, 481–82.
48. Simmel 1990 [1907], 376–80.
49. See Zelizer 2005.
50. Hochschild 2012.
51. Y. Zerubavel 1977.
52. Marx 1967 [1867], 371–465.
53. Simmel 1990 [1907], 461. Emphasis added.

Chapter 6

1. Zerubavel 2011, 19, 26.
2. Kanter 2008 [1977], 213.
3. Sofsky 1996 [1993], 216.
4. Ibid.

NOTES 83

5. Zerubavel 2015, 29.
6. Weber 1978 [1925], 242.
7. Ibid., 1114.
8. Simmel 1898, 674.
9. Weber 1978 [1925], 246, 1114.
10. Ibid., 246–49.
11. Smith 2020. Retrieved February 1, 2021.
12. Simmel 1898, 673.
13. Zerubavel 1980, 162–63; Baumann 2000, 162–63.
14. Timmermans and Epstein 2010, 71.
15. See, for example, Jutel 2009, 286–88.
16. See, for example, Knaapen 2014, 824, 829.
17. Timmermans and Berg 2003, 19.
18. Zerubavel 1993 [1991], 16–17; Zerubavel 1996.
19. Keen 1988.
20. Sumner 2007 [1906], 12.
21. Ibid.
22. See, for example, Park et al 1992; Ostrom et al. 1993; Boldry et al. 2007; K. Anderson 2010.
23. See, for example, Boldry et al. 2007, 158.
24. See, for example, Anderson 2010, 23.
25. Zerubavel 1996, 430.
26. Brooks 2021. Emphasis added. See also LaFleur 2023.
27. Hughes 1945: 357.
28. See, for example, Glaser 2015, 2–15.
29. The Associated Press, "Rights Group Challenges Israel's Airport Security." March 20, 2008. https://www.nbcnews.com/id/wbna23714853. Retrieved May 10, 2022.
30. Olson 2002.
31. See also ibid., 216, 224–28.
32. Ibid., 225. Emphasis added. See also 226.
33. See also Anderson 2010, 22–80.
34. See, for example, Timmermans and Epstein 2010, 83; Brooks 2021.
35. Weber 1978 [1925], 975.
36. Ibid., 637. Emphasis added.
37. See also Leidner 1993, 35.
38. See also ibid., 37; Lampel and Mintzberg 1996.
39. See also Karpik 2010, 19.
40. See also Lampel and Mintzberg 1996, 25–26; Piller 2004.
41. Godelier 1999 [1996], 14.

84 NOTES

42. J. Anderson 2015, 176. Emphases added.
43. See, for example, Adams and Grieder 2014.
44. See, for example, Segal and Elinav 2017.
45. See, for example, LaFleur 2023.
46. https://www.google.com/search?q=ted+koppel+iraq+nightline&rlz=1C1CHBD_enUS725US725&oq=ted+koppel+iraq+nightline&aqs=chrome..69i57j33i160j33i22i29i30l5.12736j1j15&sourceid=chrome&ie=UTF-8#fpstate=ive&vld=cid:67424e06,vid:MAnrIIg9RL8. Retrieved February1, 2023.
47. https://www.whitehouse.gov/briefing-room/press-briefings/2022/06/07/press-briefing-by-press-secretary-karine-jean-pierre-and-matthew-mcconaughey. Emphasis added. Retrieved January 27, 2023.
48. Leidner 1993, 35. Emphases added.
49. See also ibid., 12, 35; Ritzer 1996, 84, 133.
50. Hochschild 2003, 83.
51. Y. Zerubavel 1977.
52. Wheeler 2001, 74.

Bibliography

Adams, Neal, and Diane M. Grieder. *Treatment Planning for Person-Centered Care: Shared Decision Making for Whole Health.* 2nd ed. London: Academic Press, 2014.

Alicke, Mark D., and Stephanie H. Weigel. "The Reasonable Person Standard: Psychological and Legal Perspectives." *Annual Review of Law and Social Science* 17 (2021): 123–38.

Anderson, Jane. *Impact: How to Build Your Personal Brand for the Connection Economy.* Australia: Jane Anderson, 2015.

Anderson, Kristin J. *Benign Bigotry: The Psychology of Subtle Prejudice.* Cambridge, UK: Cambridge University Press, 2010.

Appelrouth, Scott, and Laura D. Edles (eds.). *Sociological Theory in the Contemporary Era: Text and Readings.* 2nd ed. Thousand Oaks, CA: Pine Forge Press, 2011.

Aristotle. *The Politics.* Chicago: University of Chicago Press, 1984 [Fourth century BC].

Baron, Joseph L. (ed.). *A Treasury of Jewish Quotations.* Lanham, MD: Rowman & Littlefield, 2004.

Bateson, Gregory. "A Theory of Play and Fantasy." In *Steps to an Ecology of Mind,* 177–93. New York: Ballantine, 1972 [1955].

Bauman, Zygmunt. *Modernity and the Holocaust.* Ithaca, NY: Cornell University Press, 2000.

Benzecry, Claudio E. *The Perfect Fit: Creative Work in the Global Shoe Industry.* Chicago: University of Chicago Press, 2022.

Berger, Peter L., and Thomas Luckmann. *The Social Construction of Reality: A Treatise in the Sociology of Knowledge.* Garden City, NY: Doubleday Anchor, 1967 [1966].

Boldry, Jennifer G., et al. "Measuring the Measures: A Meta-Analytic Investigation of the Measures of Outgroup Homogeneity." *Group Processes and Intergroup Relations* 10 (2007): 157–78.

Bray, Ilona. *Selling Your House: Nolo's Essential Guide.* Berkeley, CA: Nolo, 2019.

Brekhus, Wayne H. *Peacocks, Chameleons, Centaurs: Gay Suburbia and the Grammar of Social Identity.* Chicago: University of Chicago Press, 2003.

86 BIBLIOGRAPHY

Brooks, David. "Here's the Mind-Set That's Tearing Us Apart." *The New York Times*, October 8, 2021, A24.

Brubaker, Rogers. *The Limits of Rationality: An Essay on the Social and Moral Thought of Max Weber*. London: Allen & Unwin, 1984.

Busch, Lawrence. *Standards: Recipes for Reality*. Cambridge, MA: MIT Press, 2011.

Cohen, Patricia C. *A Calculating People: The Spread of Numeracy in Early America*. Chicago: University of Chicago Press, 1982.

Cohen, Yehudi A. "Social Boundary Systems." *Current Anthropology* 10 (1969): 103–17.

Coser, Lewis A. *Masters of Sociological Thought: Ideas in Historical and Social Context*. New York: Harcourt Brace Jovanovich, 1971.

Cox, Harvey. *The Secular City: Secularization and Urbanization in Theological Perspective*. Princeton, NJ: Princeton University Press, 2013 [1965].

Cummins, Fred. *The Ground from Which We Speak: Joint Speech and the Collective Subject*. Newcastle, UK: Cambridge Scholars, 2018a.

_____. "Joint Speech as an Object of Empirical Inquiry." *Material Religion* 14 (2018b): 417–19.

Davis, Murray S. *Smut: Erotic Reality/Obscene Ideology*. Chicago: University of Chicago Press, 1983.

DeGloma, Thomas. *Seeing the Light: The Social Logic of Personal Discovery*. Chicago: University of Chicago Press, 2014.

_____. *Anonymous: The Performance of Hidden Identities*. Chicago: University of Chicago Press, 2023.

de Swaan, Abram. *Human Societies: An Introduction*. Cambridge, UK: Polity, 2001.

Downie, R. S. "Personal and Impersonal Relationships." *Journal of Philosophy of Education* 5 (1971): 125–38.

Dubin, Steven C. "Visual Onomatopoeia." *Symbolic Interaction* 13 (1990): 185–216.

Durkheim, Emile. *Suicide: A Study in Sociology*. New York: Free Press, 1966 [1897].

_____. "The Dualism of Human Nature and Its Social Conditions." In Robert N. Bellah (ed.), *Emile Durkheim: On Morality and Society*, 149–63. Chicago: University of Chicago Press, 1973 [1914].

Emerson, Joan P. "Behavior in Private Places: Sustaining Definitions of Reality in Gynecological Examinations." In Hans-Peter Dreitzel (ed.), *Recent Sociology No. 2: Patterns of Communicative Behavior*, 74–93. London: Macmillan, 1970.

Festinger, Leon, et al. "Some Consequences of De-Individuation in a Group." *Journal of Abnormal and Social Psychology* 47 (1952): 382–89.

Flaubert, Gustave. *Madame Bovary*. Ware, UK: Wordsworth, 1994 [1856].

Foucault, Michel. *Discipline and Punish: The Birth of the Prison*. New York: Vintage Books, 1979 [1975].

BIBLIOGRAPHY 87

Fussell, Paul. *Uniforms: Why We Are What We Wear*. Boston: Houghton Mifflin, 2002.

Glaser, Jack. *Suspect Race: Causes and Consequences of Racial Profiling*. New York: Oxford University Press, 2015.

Godelier, Maurice. *The Enigma of the Gift*. Chicago: University of Chicago Press, 1999 [1996].

Goffman, Erving. "Fun in Games." In *Encounters: Two Studies in the Sociology of Interaction*, 15–81. Indianapolis, IN: Bobbs-Merrill, 1961a.

____. "Role Distance." In *Encounters: Two Studies in the Sociology of Interaction*, 83–152. Indianapolis, IN: Bobbs-Merrill, 1961b.

____. *Behavior in Public Places: Notes on the Social Organization of Gatherings*. New York: Free Press, 1963a.

____. *Stigma: Notes on the Management of Spoiled Identity*. Englewood Cliffs, NJ: Prentice-Hall, 1963b.

____. *Frame Analysis: An Essay on the Organization of Experience*. New York: Harper & Row, 1974.

Green, Joshua. "The Secret Fundraising Magic of Trump Cards." *Bloomberg Businessweek*, August 5, 2021. https://www.bloomberg.com/news/articles/2021-08-05/trump-cards-the-story-behind-the-secret-fundraising-magic.

Haberman, Maggie. "Trump Departs Vowing, 'We Will Be Back in Some Form.'" *The New York Times*, January 21, 2021. https://www.nytimes.com/2021/01/20/us/politics/trump-presidency.html.

Hall, Walter H. *The Essentials of Choir Boy Training*. New York: Novello, Ewer, & Co., 1906.

Hobbes, Thomas. *Leviathan*. London: Routledge, 2016 [1651].

Hochschild, Arlie R. *The Managed Heart: Commercialization of Human Feeling*. Berkeley: University of California Press, 1983.

____. *The Commercialization of Intimate Life: Notes from Home and Work*. Berkeley: University of California Press, 2003.

____. *The Outsourced Self: What Happens When We Pay Others to Live Our Lives for Us*. New York: Holt, 2012.

Horst, Juliana de Oliveira. "From Personal to Impersonal: Keying Strategies in the Workplace." Paper presented at the annual meeting of the American Sociological Association, Los Angeles, 2022.

Hughes, Everett C. "Dilemmas and Contradictions of Status." *American Journal of Sociology* 50 (1945): 353–59.

Humphreys, Laud. *Tearoom Trade: Impersonal Sex in Public Places*. Chicago: Aldine, 1970.

Jutel, Annemarie. "Sociology of Diagnosis: A Preliminary Review." *Sociology of Health and Illness* 31 (2009): 278–99.

Kanter, Rosabeth M. *Men and Women of the Corporation*. New York: Basic Books, 2008 [1977].

Kantorowicz, Ernst H. *The King's Two Bodies: A Study in Medieval Political Theology*. Princeton, NJ: Princeton University Press, 2016 [1957].

88 BIBLIOGRAPHY

Karpik, Lucien. *Valuing the Unique: The Economics of Singularities*. Princeton, NJ: Princeton University Press, 2010.

Keen, Sam. *Faces of the Enemy: Reflections of the Hostile Imagination*. San Francisco: Harper & Row, 1988.

Kilpatrick, Carroll. "Nixon Resigns." *The Washington Post*, August 9, 1974. https://www.washingtonpost.com/wp-srv/national/longterm/watergate/articles/080974-3.htm.

Knaapen, Loes. "Evidence-Based Medicine or Cookbook Medicine? Addressing Concerns over the Standardization of Care." *Sociology Compass* 8 (2014): 823–36.

Kolnai, Aurel. "The Meaning of the 'Common Man.'" In *Privilege and Liberty and Other Essays in Political Philosophy*, 63–104. Lanham, MD: Lexington, 1999 [1949].

LaFleur, Gabrielle. "Damaged Goods: The Sexual Assault Survivor as a Marked Identity." Paper presented at the "What People Leave Behind: Marks, Traces, Footprints, and Their Significance for the Social Sciences" conference, Rome, 2021.

——. "'Damaged Goods': Victimhood-Survivorship and the Social Marking of Identity in the 'Stanford Rape.'" Unpublished paper, Rutgers University, 2023.

Lampel, Joseph, and Henry Mintzberg. "Customizing Customization." *Sloan Management Review* (Fall 1996): 21–30.

Leidner, Robin. *Fast Food, Fast Talk: Service Work and the Routinization of Everyday Life*. Berkeley: University of California Press, 1993.

Leschziner, Vanina. *At the Chef's Table: Culinary Creativity in Elite Restaurants*. Stanford, CA: Stanford University Press, 2015.

Levin, Bess. "Trump Is Two Weeks Away from Telling Supporters to Tattoo His Face on Their Asses." *Vanity Fair*, August 5, 2021. https://www.vanityfair.com/news/2021/08/donald-trump-trump-cards.

Lévi-Strauss, Claude. *The Savage Mind*. Chicago: University of Chicago Press, 1966 [1962].

Lofland, Lyn H. *A World of Strangers: Order and Action in Urban Public Space*. New York: Basic Books, 1973.

Ludovino, Emilia M. *Emotional Intelligence for IT Professionals: The Must-Have Guide for a Successful Career in IT*. Birmingham, UK: Packt Publishing, 2017.

Maroney, Terry A. "Emotional Regulation and Judicial Behavior." *California Law Review* 99 (2011): 1485–555.

Maroney, Terry A., and James J. Gross. "The Ideal of the Dispassionate Judge: An Emotion Regulation Perspective." *Emotion Review* 6 (2014): 142–51.

Marx, Karl. *Capital, Vol. 1: A Critical Analysis of Capitalist Production*. New York: International Publishers, 1967 [1867].

Mauss, Marcel. *The Gift: Forms and Functions of Exchange in Archaic Societies*. New York: Norton, 1967 [1925].

BIBLIOGRAPHY 89

Mayntz, Renate. "The Nature and Genesis of Impersonality: Some Results of a Study on the Doctor–Patient Relationship." *Social Research* 37 (1970): 428–46.

McGregor-Wood, Simon. "Palestinian Who Claimed to Be a Jew Jailed for Rape by Deception." ABC News, July 22, 2010. https://abcnews.go.com/international/palestinian-claimed-jew-jailed-rape-deception/story?id=11224513.

McPherson, Herschel. "While Black Project." December 10, 2020. https://vimeo.com/489500564.

Mead, George H. "The Psychology of Punitive Justice." *American Journal of Sociology* 23 (1918): 577–602.

Melman, Yossi. ' "Israel Will Be Ashamed It Didn't Stand with Us,' Ukraine's Defense Minister Says." *Haaretz*, October 27, 2022. https://www.haaretz.com/israel-news/2022-10-27/ty-article-magazine/.highlight/ukraines-defense-minister-israel-will-be-ashamed-it-didnt-stand-with-us/00000184-1a63-d88a-a1e6-7f73ff150000.

Mill, John Stuart. *On Liberty*. Indianapolis, IN: Bobbs-Merrill, 1956 [1859].

Mosse, George L. *Fallen Soldiers: Reshaping the Memory of the World Wars*. New York: Oxford University Press, 1990.

Mullaney, Jamie L. "Making It 'Count': Mental Weighing and Identity Attribution." *Symbolic Interaction* 22 (1999): 269–83.

Mulvin, Dylan. *Proxies: The Cultural Work of Standing In*. Cambridge, MA: MIT Press, 2021.

Olson, Kathryn M. "Detecting a Common Interpretive Framework for Impersonal Violence: The Homology in Participants' Rhetoric on Sport Hunting, 'Hate Crimes,' and Stranger Rape." *Southern Communication Journal* 67 (2002): 215–44.

Ostrom, Thomas M., et al. "Differential Processing of In-Group and Out-Group Information." *Journal of Personality and Social Psychology* 64 (1993): 21–34.

Paris, Francesca, and Josh Katz. "Audits of Comey and McCabe: Is a Coincidence Possible?" *The New York Times*, July 8, 2022, A17.

Park, Bernadette, et al. "Role of Meaningful Subgroups in Explaining Differences in Perceived Variability for In-Groups and Out-Groups." *Journal of Personality and Social Psychology* 63 (1992): 553–67.

Parsons, Talcott. *The Social System*. New York: Free Press, 1951.

Piller, Frank T. "Mass Customization: Reflections on the State of the Concept." *International Journal of Flexible Manufacturing Systems* 16 (2004): 313–34.

Plott, Elaina. "Red-Hatted Faithful Descend, Showing Allegiance Not to Their Party but to Trump." *The New York Times*, March 1, 2021, A14.

Pollard, Danny T. *Obama Guilty of Being President While Black*. Grand Prairie, TX: Book Express, 2009.

90 BIBLIOGRAPHY

Quattrone, George A., and Edward E. Jones. "The Perception of Variability Within In-Groups and Out-Groups: Implications for the Law of Small Numbers." *Journal of Personality and Social Psychology* 38 (1980): 141–52.

Quetelet, Adolphe. *A Treatise on Man and the Development of His Faculties.* Cambridge, UK: Cambridge University Press, 2013 [1842].

Rich, Adrienne. "Compulsory Heterosexuality and Lesbian Existence." *Signs* 5 (1980): 631–60.

Ritzer, George. *The McDonaldization of Society.* Thousand Oaks, CA: SAGE, 1996.

Rosch, Eleanor H. "Principles of Categorization." In Eleanor Rosch and Barbara B. Lloyd (eds.), *Cognition and Categorization,* 27–48. Hillside, NJ: Erlbaum, 1978.

Rubin, Jennifer. "This Is Not a Normal President." *The Washington Post,* May 1, 2017. https://www.washingtonpost.com/blogs/right-turn/wp/2017/05/01/this-is-not-a-normal-president.

Saussure, Ferdinand de. *Course in General Linguistics.* New York: Philosophical Library, 1959 [1915].

Schutz, Alfred. *The Phenomenology of the Social World.* Evanston, IL: Northwestern University Press, 1967 [1932].

Schutz, Alfred, and Thomas Luckmann. *The Structures of the Life-World.* Evanston, IL: Northwestern University Press, 1973.

Schwartz, Barry. "The Social Psychology of the Gift." *American Journal of Sociology* 73 (1967): 1–11.

Segal, Eran, and Eran Elinav. *The Personalized Diet: The Pioneering Program to Lose Weight and Prevent Disease.* New York: Grand Central Publishing, 2017.

Simmel, Georg. "The Persistence of Social Groups." *American Journal of Sociology* 3 (1898): 662–98.

———. "The Metropolis and Mental Life." In Kurt H. Wolff (ed.), *The Sociology of Georg Simmel,* 409–24. New York: Free Press, 1950 [1903].

———. *The Philosophy of Money.* 2nd ed. London: Routledge, 1990 [1907].

———. "The Quantitative Determination of Group Divisions and of Certain Groups." In Kurt H. Wolff (ed.), *The Sociology of Georg Simmel,* 105–17. New York: Free Press, 1950 [1908a].

———. "Superordination and Subordination." In Kurt H. Wolff (ed.), *The Sociology of Georg Simmel,* 179–303. New York: Free Press, 1950 [1908b].

———. "Types of Social Relationships by Degrees of Reciprocal Knowledge of Their Participants." In Kurt H. Wolff (ed.), *The Sociology of Georg Simmel,* 317–29. New York: Free Press, 1950 [1908c].

———. "Written Communication." In Kurt H. Wolff (ed.), *The Sociology of Georg Simmel,* 352–55. New York: Free Press, 1950 [1908d].

———. "Excursus on Hereditary Office." In *Sociology: Inquiries into the Construction of Social Forms,* 461–68. Leiden, The Netherlands: Brill, 2009 [1908].

BIBLIOGRAPHY   91

_____. "Sociability." In Kurt H. Wolff (ed.), *The Sociology of Georg Simmel*, 40-57. New York: Free Press, 1950 [1917].

Simpson, Ruth. "The Germ Culture." PhD dissertation, Rutgers University, 2006.

Šmídová, Olga, and Blanka Tollarová. "'You Can't Take It Personally': Emotion Management as Part of the Professional Nurse's Role." *Czech Sociological Review* 50 (2014): 839–73.

Smith, Rory. "There Will Never Be a New Maradona." *The New York Times*, November 29, 2020, A32.

Sofsky, Wolfgang. *The Order of Terror: The Concentration Camp*. Princeton, NJ: Princeton University Press, 1996 [1993].

Sommers, Roseanna. "You Were Duped Into Saying Yes. Is It Still Consent?" *The New York Times*, March 6, 2021, A23.

Sorokin, Pitirim A. *Sociocultural Causality, Space, Time: A Study of Referential Principles of Sociology and Social Science*. Durham, NC: Duke University Press, 1943.

Spencer, Herbert. *Principles of Sociology*. Hamden, CT: Archon, 1969 [1876].

Steinberg, Ronnie J., and Deborah M. Figart. "Emotional Labor Since *The Managed Heart*." *Annals of the American Academy of Political and Social Science* 561 (1999): 8–26.

Strong, Carol, and Matt Killingsworth. "Stalin the Charismatic Leader? Explaining the 'Cult of Personality' as a Legitimating Technique." *Politics, Religion, and Ideology* 12 (2011): 391–411.

Stubbs, William. *The Constitutional History of England in Its Origin and Development, Vol. 3*. Cambridge, UK: Cambridge University Press, 1878.

Styron, William. *Sophie's Choice*. New York: Random House, 1979.

Sumner, William G. *Folkways: A Study of Mores, Manners, Customs, and Morals*. New York: Cosimo, 2007 [1906].

Suro, Roberto. "John Paul Holds Waldheim Meeting." *The New York Times*, June 26, 1987, A1, A4. https://timesmachine.nytimes.com/timesmachine/1987/06/26/469987.html.

Tajfel, Henri. *Human Groups and Social Categories: Studies in Social Psychology*. New York: Cambridge University Press, 1981.

Tajfel, Henri, and John C. Turner. "The Social Identity Theory in Intergroup Behavior." In Stephen Worchel and William G. Austin (eds.), *Psychology of Intergroup Relations*, 7–24. Chicago: Nelson-Hall, 1986.

Timmermans, Stefan, and Marc Berg. *The Gold Standard: The Challenge of Evidence-Based Medicine and Standardization in Health Care*. Philadelphia: Temple University Press, 2003.

Timmermans, Stefan, and Steven Epstein. "A World of Standards but Not a Standard World: Toward a Sociology of Standards and Standardization." *Annual Review of Sociology* 36 (2010): 69–89.

Tocqueville, Alexis de. *Democracy in America, Vol. 1*. New York: Vintage Books, 1945 [1835].

92 BIBLIOGRAPHY

Toffler, Alvin. *Future Shock*. New York: Bantam, 1974 [1970].

Turkle, Sherry. *Life on the Screen: Identity in the Age of the Internet*. New York: Simon & Schuster, 1995.

Wallis, John J. "Institutions, Organizations, Impersonality, and Interests: The Dynamics of Institutions." *Journal of Economic Behavior and Organization* 79 (2011): 48–64.

Watt, Ian. *The Rise of the Novel: Studies in Defoe, Richardson, and Fielding*. Berkeley: University of California Press, 2001 [1957].

Weber, Max. "'Objectivity' in Social Science and Social Policy." In *The Methodology of the Social Sciences*, 49–112. New York: Free Press, 1949 [1904].

———. *The Protestant Ethic and the Spirit of Capitalism*. New York: Charles Scribner's Sons, 1958 [1904–05].

———. *Economy and Society*. Berkeley: University of California Press, 1978 [1925].

Wheeler, Linda A. *Ain't Life a Pomegranate?* Honolulu, Hawaii: The Human Connection, 2001.

Wirth, Louis. "Urbanism as a Way of Life." *American Journal of Sociology* 44 (1938): 1–24.

Zelizer, Viviana A. "Payments and Social Ties." *Sociological Forum* 11 (1996): 481–95.

———. *The Purchase of Intimacy*. Princeton, NJ: Princeton University Press, 2005.

———. "Circuits Within Capitalism." In *Economic Lives: How Culture Shapes the Economy*, 311–43. Princeton, NJ: Princeton University Press, 2011 [2005].

Zerubavel, Eviatar. *Patterns of Time in Hospital Life: A Sociological Perspective*. Chicago: University of Chicago Press, 1979.

———. "The Bureaucratization of Responsibility: The Case of Informed Consent." *Bulletin of the American Academy of Psychiatry and the Law* 8 (1980): 161–67.

———. "The Standardization of Time: A Sociohistorical Perspective." *American Journal of Sociology* 88 (1982), 1–23.

———. *The Fine Line: Making Distinctions in Everyday Life*. Chicago: University of Chicago Press, 1993 [1991].

———. "Lumping and Splitting: Notes on Social Classification." *Sociological Forum* 11 (1996): 421–33.

———. *Social Mindscapes: An Invitation to Cognitive Sociology*. Cambridge, MA: Harvard University Press, 1997.

———. *Ancestors and Relatives: Genealogy, Identity, and Community*. New York: Oxford University Press, 2011.

———. *Hidden in Plain Sight: The Social Structure of Irrelevance*. New York: Oxford University Press, 2015.

———. *Taken for Granted: The Remarkable Power of the Unremarkable*. Princeton, NJ: Princeton University Press, 2018.

BIBLIOGRAPHY   93

____. *Generally Speaking: An Invitation to Concept-Driven Sociology.* New York: Oxford University Press, 2021.

Zerubavel, Yael. "Greeting Cards." Paper presented at the annual meeting of the American Folklore Society, Detroit, 1977.

____. *Recovered Roots: Collective Memory and the Making of Israeli National Tradition.* Chicago: University of Chicago Press, 1995.

____. "'Numerical Commemoration' and the Challenges of Collective Remembrance in Israel." *History and Memory* 26 (2014): 5–38.

Index

For the benefit of digital users, indexed terms that span two pages (e.g., 52–53) may, on occasion, appear on only one of those pages.

aggregate numbers, 14–15, 70
anonymity, 30, 45–46, 54–56, 58, 70
anonymization, 43–46
any, 7, 30, 34, 37, 39–42, 45, 48
anyone, 8, 45, 47, 50, 53, 57, 70
"anyoneness", 8, 29, 53
archetypes, 4
aristocracy, 18
Aristotle, 18
arithmetic: political, 16–18;
   social, 12–21
arithmetical vision of
   personhood, 13–15
arithmetized individual, the, 19
atypicality, 26, 32
automation, x, 58–59, 64, 68–69
authority: charismatic, 5–6, 37, 62–63;
   hereditary, 39, 42;
   impersonal, 35–38, 45, 64;
   legal, 37–38, 40;
   traditional, 39–40;
   transferring, 39–40, 43
"average man", the, 34

backgrounding, 32, 34, 48, 69. *See also*
   foregrounding
being versus doing, 22
Benzecry, Claudio, 57
blasé attitude, 54. *See also* dispassion
Brooks, David, 61
bureaucracy, 16, 37, 39, 41, 47, 52–53, 56, 59
bureaucratization, 11, 52

capitalism, 56–57, 59, 68–69

capping, 16
categories, 3, 8–9, 13, 15, 25–27, 29–30, 32–34, 41, 58, 61, 65–66;
   generic, 3, 8–9, 34, 41, 51;
   membership in, 3, 8–9, 15, 25–27, 29–30, 32, 41, 58, 65–68;
   social, 8, 25–27, 29–30, 32, 58, 65–68
celebrity, 5, 29
charisma, ix, 5–6, 26, 29, 32, 35–37, 39, 62–64;
   attributing, 5–6, 27, 62–63;
   hereditary, 39–40;
   transferring, 39
choice, personal, 8, 14, 69
commercial versus personal
   relations, 58–59
commodification, 11, 56–57
"*cookbook*" medicine, 65, 70
"*cookie cutter*", 70
Coser, Lewis, 10
counting versus weighing, 14, 16–17, 19
cult of personality, 6, 64
customization, 57, 69

de-eroticization, 49–50
DeGloma, Thomas, 45–47
dehumanization, 61, 68
de-identifying, 46
de-individuation, 24, 33, 43–46
democracy, 17–19
depersonalization, 45, 47, 56, 68
de-singularization, 33–34
diagnosing, 33, 59, 65
dispassion, 47–49, 52, 54–55, 59

96 INDEX

distinctiveness, 4–5, 14, 23, 25, 30, 35, 41, 44–45, 65–66, 69–70, 73
"*Don't take it personally*", ix, 7, 55, 73
Durkheim, Emile, 9, 78

egalitarianism, 17, 19, 34–35
elitism, 18
equality, arithmetical, 17
ex cathedra, 38
exceptionality, 5, 38
ex officio, 38
expectations, standard, 25, 27, 47–48, 58
extraordinariness, 5, 62

facelessness, 30, 34
"*featured*" performer, 64
Festinger, Leon, 24
filling in for, 41
fitting, 38, 57, 69
foregrounding, 7, 14, 24, 32, 34, 66, 69. *See also* backgrounding
formulaicness, 28, 35–36, 58, 72–73
Foucault, Michel, 44
fraction, social, 19–20
friendship, 5, 7, 26, 29, 47, 72

generalization, 26, 34, 51
generically, 8–10, 12, 19, 25, 29, 43, 51, 61, 65–66
generic individuals, 3
genericity, 3, 7, 51, 69
genericization, 32–33
gifting, 1, 30, 46, 58, 69–70
Goffman, Erving, 23
greeting card, 58–59, 72–73
group, social, 20, 25–27, 32, 65
group membership, 4, 13, 17–19, 25–27, 30, 32, 41, 43–44, 51, 65, 68
groupness, 43–45

handwriting, 72
hate crime, 67–68
head count, 13
Her, 60, 72
Hobbes, Thomas, 48
Hochschild, Arlie, 58, 72
homogenizing out-groups, 65–68
"how-many-based": decisions, 18;

identity, 13;
social cognition, 12

identifiability, 21, 25, 29, 31, 43, 45–46, 64, 67, 71
identification, 7, 23, 65, 66
identity: "damaged", 24;
group-centric, 25;
marked, 24, 26;
personal, 2, 7–8, 13, 23–24, 30, 32, 35, 41, 43, 45–46, 55, 67, 69–70;
social, 2, 13, 23–26, 32, 66, 69;
stigmatized, 24, 26
idiosyncrasy, 3–4, 14, 33–35, 44, 51, 57, 65, 69
"I'm Just a Dancing Partner", 3, 23
impartiality, 27, 47–48
"imperson", 7, 59
impersonal: considerations, 8;
decisions, 13;
relations, 3, 49, 53, 56, 58;
violence, 67;
vision of personhood, 20, 37, 55
impersonality, 3, 7–11, 21–22, 25, 27–29, 32, 34–35, 43–44, 47, 51–56, 60–61, 63–64, 70, 73;
benefits of, 61–62, 64;
costs of, 9, 64
impersonalization, 4, 32–33, 35–37, 45–47, 49, 52, 55, 57, 59, 63, 68–69, 71;
of authority, 35–36;
of modern life, 52, 59
impersonally, 3, 9, 13, 20, 25–26, 30, 38, 41, 46, 62, 64
improvisation, 28, 70
inconspicuity, 62. *See also* anonymity
incumbent of a role, 7, 25, 27–29, 31, 38, 40, 42, 64. *See also* occupant of a position
individuality, 18, 43–44, 65, 68, 70
individualization, 65, 70
instability, 36, 63
in step, 44
institutionalization, 36–41, 52
interchangeability, 29–30, 39, 41, 56, 58, 65–67
in unison, 44–45
irreplaceability, 39

INDEX 97

Jefferson, Thomas, 17
job description, 9, 38
job search, 8–9, 36, 38, 66
joint speech, 44–45

Kanter, Rosabeth, 20

labeling, 33, 66
language, 51, 61
law, impersonal spirit of the, ix, 8, 25, 27–28, 35, 37
Leidner, Robin, 72
"leveling", political, 17
libertarianism, 18
lines in a play, 41
Lofland, Lyn, 54
love, 4, 26, 28–29, 47–48, 58, 60
loyalty, personal, 6–7, 37

machines, 59–60, 68–69
Madame Bovary, 4
majority, 18, 20;
    tyranny of the, 18
majority rule, 17–19
market, the, 56
marketization, 11, 55, 68
Marx, Karl, 56, 59
mass production, 66–67, 69, 73
mavericks, 35
maximum number of persons, 15–16
Mayntz, Renate, 22
Mill, John Stuart, 18
minimum number of persons, 15
minority, 18–20
modernity, 51–59, 65, 68–69
money, 57–59
monogrammed jewelry, 73
"My Way", 6

name, 1, 3, 9, 25, 46, 55, 58, 70–71
name badge, 70, 72
name conflation, 65–66
namelessness, 30–31, 55. *See also* anonymity
neutrality, 33;
    affective, 47
Night and Fog, 64–65
non-identifiability, 46

non-personcentric rules, 8, 61
nonstandardness, 38, 70
"*nothing personal*", ix, 7, 47, 55, 73
numerical commemoration, 19–20
numerically designated collective entities, 13, 19–20
numerus clausus, 16

objectifying, 68
objectivity, 47–48, 52–53, 57
occupant: of an office, 42;
    of a position, ix, 10, 24, 27, 29, 31, 38–43, 51
office, 37–38, 42
Olson, Kathryn, 68
"*out of step*", 44
outsourcing, 58–59, 72
outvoting, 17, 19

Parsons, Talcott, 47–48
particular individuals, 3, 5, 7–8, 12–13, 17, 20, 30, 38, 48, 62, 65, 67
particularization, 4
peculiarity, individual, 14
per capita, 16
persona, public, 22–23
personal identitylessness, 34
personalization, 23, 35, 69–73
personally, ix, 3, 5, 7, 9, 13, 25, 29–31, 38, 46, 48, 54, 56, 62, 70, 73
personalness, 3–5, 7, 9–11, 21–22, 25–27, 35, 47–48, 52, 60, 62–64, 69–73
personal qualities, 25, 37, 39, 53
"*personal touch*", 69, 72
personal vision of personhood, 4–6, 37
personcentricity, 3–6, 8–9, 14, 21, 25, 27–31, 36–40, 46, 49, 51, 57–58, 60–61, 63–65, 67–70, 72
personhood, ix, 3–6, 9–17, 20, 32, 37, 52, 54–55, 59, 66, 73
personification, 43, 60, 68
person-to-"imperson" transaction, 59
plurality, 20
"*plus one*", 19
position, ix, 6, 10, 15, 24, 27, 31, 35–43, 48, 51, 53;
    institutional, 42;
    social, 39, 43

98 INDEX

precedent, legal, 34
predictability, 27, 64
prejudice, 66–67
procedure, 28, 35–36, 40, 47
professionalism, 35–36, 38, 47–49
"profile", 8
"profiling", 67
protocol, 28, 35, 65
proxy, 34, 45
pseudonym, 46
pseudo-personalization, 72–73
pseudo-personalness, 72
punishment, collective, 30, 68

qua, 23–25, 38, 67
qualitative view of personhood, 14, 17, 19
quantitative vision of personhood, 14, 16–17, 19
quantity versus "quality", 15, 18
Quetelet, Adolphe, 34
quorum, 15
quotas, 15–16

randomization, 13, 46, 70
rarity, 20
rationalism, 52–53, 56
"reasonable person", 34
replaceability, 39, 41
replacement, 39
representativeness, 7, 24, 26–27, 30, 32, 34, 41, 67–68
responsibility: collective, 30; "floating", 64; impersonal, 41, 64
Ritzer, George, 56
robocall, x, 68
roboticness, 64, 68
role, social, 7, 9, 24–25, 27–29, 42, 61, 64
romantic relations, 4, 8, 34, 49–50, 60
routine, 7, 28, 35
routinization, 35–36, 39, 72
rules, 5, 8, 27–28

"Say Their Names", 70
Schutz, Alfred, 32
scriptedness, 9, 28–29, 35, 38, 41, 68, 72
"secret Santa", 46
signature, 4, 23

Simmel, Georg, 11, 13, 17–18, 29–30, 42, 50, 54, 56–57, 59
singling out, 13, 24, 62
singularity, ix, 3–5, 9, 21, 23, 25–26, 29–30, 32–34, 43–44, 51, 69–70, 73; transcending, 10, 51, 61
singularizability, 62, 67
singularization, 4–5, 62, 70–71
Sir, 1
"*slot in the social structure*", 29, 39–40, 42
social kiss, 49
socio-arithmetical logic, 15–16
sociologists, 10–11, 24, 36
sociology, ix, 10, 20, 22, 29, 42–43, 50
"someoneness", 8, 39, 46
Sophie's Choice, 14
specialness, 5, 38
specifically, 5, 7, 9, 12–14, 31–32, 40, 43, 46, 49, 56–57, 61, 64, 67, 69, 72
specific individual, 3–5, 7–10, 13–15, 20, 23–27, 29–30, 32, 34, 38, 40–43, 45, 48, 50–51, 53, 61–62, 65–68, 70, 73
specificity, 3, 7, 32, 34, 69
specific personhood, 6–7, 13, 33, 37, 45, 72
Spencer, Herbert, 43
stability, 63
standard adjudication procedure, 35–36
standardization, 34–36, 52, 64
standardized, 16, 34–36, 58, 70, 72; career, 38; credentials, 36; production, 38, 56–57, 73; protocol, 65; tests, 36
standardness, 27–29, 34–36, 38, 52, 57, 59, 64–65, 68–69
stand-in, 20, 34
statistics, 14, 53
stereotype, 20, 26, 61, 66
stereotypification, 66
Stubbs, William, 37
subjectivity, 53–54, 57
substitutability, interpersonal, 29–31, 39, 41, 52–53, 58–59, 64
succession, 6, 39, 43, 63; line of, 39–40
symbolic immortality, 42–43

synecdoche, social, 27. *See also*
  representativeness

tailoring, 57, 69–70
Tajfel, Henri, 25
The American President, 1–2
"*They all look alike*", 68
Tocqueville, Alexis de, 18
Toffler, Alvin, 54
togetherness, 30, 45
Triumph of the Will, 44
trust, 55, 67
turnovers, 41
Twelve Angry Men, 17
type, 26–27
typicality, 27, 30, 32–35, 64–68
typification, 32–34, 51, 61, 66

uniform, 44
uniformity, 27–28, 44
uniformization, 35
uniqueness, 4–5, 23, 25, 27, 32–35,
  45, 65, 70

unpredictability, 35–36, 64
unscriptedness, 41
unspecified individuals, 3–4, 31
urbanization, 11, 53–55

Watt, Ian, 4
Weber, Max, 5–6, 11, 35, 37, 47, 51–52,
  55, 62, 68
"what-based": decisions, 18;
  identity, 12;
  social cognition, 12
"*while Black*", 24
"who-based": identity, 13;
  personhood, 12;
  social cognition, 12
"who" versus "how many", 12–21
"who" versus "what", 1–11
Wirth, Louis, 54
written documents, 41–42, 45

You've Got Mail, 55

Zerubavel, Yael, 19–20